STORIES
AND
MUSINGS

Sean A O'Reilly

authorHOUSE®

AuthorHouse™ UK
1663 Liberty Drive
Bloomington, IN 47403 USA
www.authorhouse.co.uk
Phone: 0800 047 8203 (Domestic TFN)
       +44 1908 723714 (International)

Published by AuthorHouse   08/06/2019

ISBN: 978-1-7283-9121-2 (sc)
ISBN: 978-1-7283-9120-5 (hc)
ISBN: 978-1-7283-9122-9 (e)

Print information available on the last page.

Any people depicted in stock imagery provided by Getty Images are models,
and such images are being used for illustrative purposes only.
Certain stock imagery © Getty Images.

This book is printed on acid-free paper.

Because of the dynamic nature of the Internet, any web addresses or links contained in
this book may have changed since publication and may no longer be valid. The views
expressed in this work are solely those of the author and do not necessarily reflect the
views of the publisher, and the publisher hereby disclaims any responsibility for them.

about:

Our Cat, brown bread and real ale, people and nations, biking and marathon running and other matters.

Introduction

This is a collection of short narratives of some of my life's encounters with people both socially and in sports events. Life cannot exist without food and drink and so naturally, a few stories on bread, cheese and the amber nectar get an airing. Work and play feature greatly in our lives and I have included some of my contributions, hopefully positive ones, from my life's travails.

Finally for many people the family pet animal is very important to their well being so our now deceased but amazing Billy the cat gets his own story.

Feel free to select a story in any order that catches the eye and I hope it relates maybe to some of the reader's own experiences.

Contents

FOOD FOR THOUGHT

ACROSS BORDERS

TWO WHEELS BETTER THAN ONE

LIFE'S SURPRISES

ON THE RUN

FOOD FOR THOUGHT

What's Not to Like
About Pepper

Not a day passes without hearing about a research project claiming that another food product can cause cancer. Often a few years later another research project claims the same food product actually is good for you. A glass of wine or two a day was once deemed beneficial, now it is claimed all alcohol, whatever the amount, is bad for you. Eggs, once bad, are now good for you. Even the greatest enemy of the health police – saturated fat – is now deemed in some cases to be beneficial. The latest war waged by the health police is against sugar.

There is one product that has so far escaped the researchers' carcinogenic claims, namely, my beloved pepper. The only reference on the internet that I found claimed that pepper might be carcinogenic if injected in large quantities into rats. Yes, I know mice and rats have a hard time in the researchers' torture labs. In fact, pepper's antioxidant, anti-inflammatory and anti-bacterial benefits may help to stop the development of cancer rather than cause it.

I just love freshly ground black pepper on big fleshy tomatoes, mashed turnips, pasta and on homemade squash and tomato soups. Sadly, pepper can do nothing for those horrible tasteless Dutch glasshouse grown tomatoes. Pepper, the king of spices in medieval times, is heralded for its therapeutic and medicinal value. It is claimed to aid digestion and to stimulate the spleen to produce new blood cells and to be an effective anti viral agent. Pepper oil is sometimes used by physiotherapists in massage to encourage suppleness after strenuous exercise or to ease aching muscles.

In my quest for the perfect pepper mill, I must have gone through a score of useless pepper mills over the years. I realise that the black pepper corn may be a tough nut to crack, but there is nothing more irritating than having to use a useless pepper mill in a restaurant or at home. I think I may have at last found the holy grail of pepper mills - an electric driven mill. The only problem is that it uses 6 AAA batteries, but has the advantage that I need to use it regularly to get the value for my investment in the batteries – pepper heaven as it were.

Pepper has made it into children's fairytales in the stories of the Norwegian folk musician and author Alf Proysen. Mrs Pepperpot has the magic ability to shrink to the size of a pepper pot but has to keep her teaspoon, which is normal size. The pepper pot sized woman is able to survive her adventures as she can speak the languages of the small animal world. The Japanese produced a successful animation cartoon series of Mrs Pepperpot's adventures. Towards the end of the series it was revealed that Mr Pepperpot found out about his wife's secret – oh Dear!

Who would have thought that pepper could be of more use as a defence weapon than a handgun and with far less legal implications in its deployment. Regulations on carrying pepper spray aerosols vary from country to country. Some countries actively encourage the use of regulated pepper spray, especially by women and people in danger of being attacked by wild animals. Most national police forces carry a pepper spray device. I still would like to try using one on my wife's excellent Squash and Tomato soups – could be a solution to my pepper grinder problem – but I do not think my wife should be around when I experiment.

Some years ago my then school secretary gave me a recipe that used a lot of pepper where a hammer rather than a grinder was the selected pepper corn smasher. It was a simple and easy to prepare recipe: pasta - preferable tagliartelle, crème fraiche, salmon trimmings and pepper. Mix the freshly strained cooked tagliarelle and crème fraiche into a preheated pan and stir well. Then fine cut and stir in the salmon trimmings and now for the good bit. Put a small handful of black pepper corns into a cloth bag and then crush them with a good blow of the hammer. Mix and stir in the coarsely crushed pepper into the tagliatelle mix and serve immediately whilst still hot. Serve with a quality lager beer. Hey presto — delicious.

My fixation with freshly ground black pepper to date has not allowed me to experiment with white pepper – made from the ripe pepper seed. Equally, I have not tried green pepper made from the unripe fruit. That is something to look forward to in the future. There is also pink pepper, not related to real pepper which grows on trees in California and other places which is popular in Germany. Incidentally a rich man in Germany is often called a 'pfeffer sack' which goes back to medieval times when a lot of money was made by some merchants dealing in spices.

Pass the pepper please.

Brown Bread Rolls –Say No to White Bread

Not rolling off the shelves; not even on the shelves

I just love a fresh crusty wholemeal or granary brown bread roll. The problem is that they are increasingly hard to come by, at least in the UK. Recently in my local large TESCO store, I could not find a single brown roll of any sort amid a sea of white bread of all shapes and sizes and a lot of it sliced and wrapped in plastic bags.

It is presently estimated that about 20% of the population is obese. Could it be that the 12 million mostly white loaves sold each day are a contributory factor? White bread has a lot less fibre than brown and has a quicker energy release, so one can feel hunger pangs not too longer after eating. This is the reason why I also prefer oat porridge in the morning, because of its slower energy release and high fibre content.

We need to go back to the early 20C to find the reason why white bread is so popular. Before the First World War only the white core of wheat was used and the rest discarded or used for animal feed. During this war, the German submarines were attacking merchant ships carrying wheat to the UK. This soon resulted in the UK having to rely on homegrown wheat. "Waste not want not" became a popular slogan of the war. Soon the British Bread Order of 1917 was enforced whereby bread less than 12 hours old could not be sold in the shops. The idea was to reduce consumption and this worked by allowing the slightly stale and stiffer bread to be cut into thinner slices for sale. It also meant that as most of the bakers were now women – more and more men were recruited into the army and baking could be done during the day saving on lighting and heating and allowing the women to be at home with their children in the evenings. Only a generation later, the exercise was repeated to cope in the Second World War. In 1942, the government introduced the "wholemeal loaf" decreeing that the whole wheat grain including the husks be included. This resulted in a heavy beige coloured and gritty in texture loaf – not at all popular with the populace who saw it as nasty, dry, dank and indigestible, but still better than nothing. This was more galling to them as they again had got accustomed to consuming their favourite white loaf. In addition, technology had moved on when in 1928 the bread slicer was invented in the US and by 1933, nearly 80% of all bread was sold wrapped and sliced and 50% of bread eaten was in the form of sandwiches and most of it white. It is not surprising the saying "the best thing since sliced bread" entered the language.

It was the upper classes, with their prawn and cucumber sandwiches, that lead the war against brown and crusty bread. When the village clock struck three the well heeled sat down for afternoon tea. No one would dare to have his or her white bread slices with the crust not cut off. This tradition still exists today in London hotels like the Ritz and the Savoy where you can pay £50 a head to have your dainty crustless white sandwiches. They are invariable accompanied with over refined and sugared near fibreless cakes.

The ultimate sin in the bread bin world is the wrapping of nearly all bread in non-recyclable thin plastic bags or Clingfilm that can end up in our oceans causing serious damage to fish and bird life across the globe. At least when you buy bread rolls there is normally a paper bag for them; but alas these are now being replaced by, you guessed it, thin Clingfilm like plastic bags. We still have time to follow the French who are quite happy to receive their daily Baguette from the Boulangerie without a bag or just a band of paper if you are the fussy type.

Every year I look forward going skiing in Austria where I can join the queue at my local Backerei for expensive but wonderful brown crusty rolls served with a smile and in paper bags. Even the local supermarket serves up a great variety of bread made from a mix of cereals. If you want the ultimate antidote to white bread, you can go for the Schwarzbrot, a very dark brown bread made of whole rye grains.

For years now my local Coop has been recording how many and what type of rolls are sold each day. You can get four rolls costing only a £1, which is great value. When you arrive at the till the shop assistant takes out a chart and keys in the number and type of roll one has bought. This can take some time but the idea is to help the bakery to estimate how much dough they need to prepare each day. When I first starting buying my rolls at the Coop there were nearly always two good quality types of brown rolls available throughout the day. Recently I was shocked to find that on many occasions there were no brown rolls of any kind available, only white. It turned out that they had not baked any in response to almost zero demand from the customers. It was the same story at our large new Sainsbury's and Tesco stores. I think I have lost the war on behalf of the brown roll.

Supermarkets and other bread outlets are getting it badly wrong when it comes to judging our daily bread needs. Nearly 45% of production is wasted, that is 2.5 million slices a day. Some of it is used for cattle feed, compost and for food banks. The more unusual uses include making Craft Toast Ale that uses 10 kgm of bread for every 100 litres of ale brewed. The Campaign for Real Bread may help to stem some of the wastage and educate the people on the benefits of real bread in stemming obesity and diabetes. We live in hope.

In the meantime, I will resort again to baking my own crusty Irish Soda Bread. Ingredients: wholemeal flour, Flahavans Irish Oats, buttermilk and a knob of Kerrygold butter with a dash of salt and a heaped teaspoon of bicarbonate of soda. It goes well with fresh homemade jam or cheddar cheese. For the more adventurous, it is a delightful accompaniment to Guinness and Oysters.

Slainte

Cheese and
Biscuits – Please

Most people are familiar with a Pizza Quattro Formaggi with a selection of four cheeses say mozzarella, gorgonzola, brie and ricotta. If you sprinkle parmesan on top then technically you have a five-cheese pizza. The year 2017 for me was the year of the three cheeses when my wife and I visited the homes of Wensleydale, Roquefort and Cheddar. This occurred more by accident than design.

The first of our cheeses was served up on the way up to Ayrshire, Scotland in March. In our recently acquired Hymer motor home, we drove through Wensleydale in North Yorkshire and visited the Wensleydale Creamery in Hawes. The company only uses milk sourced from local dairy farmers and the cheese has a creamy delicate taste with a nice crumbly texture. At one stage, the company was close to liquidation but was saved when selected as being the favourite cheese of Wallace in the Wallace and Grommet cartoon series. Seemingly, the owner of the creamery only found out one Christmas Eve that the cheese was going to feature big time in the series – a very happy Christmas indeed as the series created a boom in the sale of the cheese. Apparently, the cheese was selected because it allowed the creator to give easier mouth movement in the plasticine models when it was pronounced by Wallace one of the main figurines.

Our Second cheese course was served up when we called in on Roquefort in the south of France in October. The area is famous for its limestone rocks and associated caves. The caves are used to mature this world famous sheep cheese. Surprisingly we never saw a single sheep on the surrounding hills but we did see several sheep sculptures. We had a tour of the Society de Roquefort caves and as the French guide made no allowance for the only two English speakers in the group I spent my time counting the number of stored loaves of cheeses in the different caves – there were no sheep to count – so I did not fall asleep. The cheese with its penicillin formed blue veins, made from unpasteurised Ewes milk is moist, slightly crumbly, salty and very tasty. I was surprised how much salt they used in the cheese making process. Roquefort has 1.7 gm per 100gm compared to 0.75 gm in Blue Stilton its English competitor. It was the first cheese in France to gain AOC status in 1925.

Our third cheese plate served up was my favourite Cheddar. We took our first ever winter camping short holiday to the Mendip Hills in north Somerset in mid November and biked from the campsite the 8 miles or so down to Cheddar and later had the challenge of cycling back up home through the famous Cheddar George. We visited the only Cheddar cheese made in the original village of Cheddar and delighted in seeing the piles of salt shovelled into the big tank. We tasted several different types of cheddar – some of it matured in the nearby Cheddar caves.

I cannot stand cold cheese and I am horrified just how many restaurants serve up cheese directly from the fridge and with cold rock hard butter. I have resorted to ordering my cheese and biscuits – not always on the menu – as soon as I enter the restaurant. In the 1980s, I remember a hotel that I stayed in and located in the Peak District putting the cheeses out at 4pm to have it at room temperature for evening dinner, but sadly the safety and health brigade put an end to that practice. The pub traditional Ploughman's lunch is invariably served with not quite freezing cheddar but the warmish real ale helps to heat it up a bit and give it some taste. At least the ploughmen of old had their cheddar well aerated and at farmhouse or field temperature.

I hate to think how restaurants and pubs store their cheese. Probably rapped in flavour suffocating plastic cling film or worse unwrapped. I have learnt that aluminium foil is a good wrapping material for Roquefort and Stilton and waxed paper helps to stop cheddar from drying out and absorbing the flavours of other foodstuffs in the fridge. Whilst beer goes well with hard cheeses like Cheddar and Edam I prefer a good red wine with soft cheeses like Camembert and Brie. For me these cheeses have to be well matured and even a bit runny and definitely at room temperature. A final point: I like my cheeses to have a distinctive aroma – the smellier the better; but with one exception – goat cheese. Unfortunately goat cheese at times smells of the goat itself but I note people not familiar with farmed or mountain goats, especially urban folk, do not seem to be effected by the smell.

Bon Appetite.

A Walk to my Local Pub

When it comes to imbibing the amber nectar the human race can be divided into three categories: the regular drinker, the occasional drinker and the teetotaller. The latter category include those of a particular religious persuasion like Methodists or Muslims and those for health or other reasons who cannot stand the idea of drinking anything alcoholic. The occasional pub drinkers often include ramblers, holiday binge drinkers who cannot resist cheap alcohol abroad, people who never buy their round and some of those who attend weddings and funerals, where others pay for their booze. The regular drinkers include those who buy their rounds, bores who always drink the same real ale or lager and those who are prepared to drink Guinness, wine, ale, lager and spirits in any combination. Luckily, for me my relatives and friends mostly fall into the latter group.

After many trials and errors over the years, I have finally come to recognise my ideal pub, be it in country or urban back street. It will have a few well-kept draught real ales, good Guinness and a tasty pie or ploughman at the ready. It will have a smallish bar room or two and TV only on very special sporting occasions. No large dining tables but plenty of bar stools and long back benches, a wood or coal fire, a friendly established landlord or landlady and above all regular social drinkers who are willing to engage in conversation with locals and visitors – even if they talk baloney most of the time. A bonus would be occasional folk music sessions.

Sadly, such pubs are decreasing in number, replaced by impersonal gastro pubs or demolished for flats or houses because of the value of the land they occupy. They also have to struggle against cheap supermarket beer and spirits which encourages drinking at home aided by the opportunity to watch wall to wall TV sport coverage and TV box sets.

By great coincidence, I have two of my dream pubs close to home, one called "The Woodman" in countryside within two miles of my home. I can walk there on a dedicated country path. The other is called "The White Horse" in the county town of Hertford and less than a mile from my front door.

In this age of the internet and instant social media contact, why do we still need and use pubs? You can get much cheaper alcoholic drinks in the local supermarket and drink at home. The recent proliferation of coffee bars indicates that many people prefer to be on their wifi or just with a friend rather than engaging with strangers or even locals in a pub.

Historically pubs provided a meeting place for friends because their homes were too small, unheated and overcrowded. The surge in Victorian new pubs with their high ornate ceilings, warm welcoming fireplaces and mirrored walls must have felt almost cathedral like compared to the small and often damp terraced houses or cold farm cottages. Their royal names: Old Vic, New Vic, King's Head, Queen's Arms, added to their mystic in the eyes of the growing urban working class. Country pubs were smaller and reflected the occupation of their clientele: The Woodman, The Plough, Farmer's Boy, The Black Horse, Pig and Whistle.

Conversation at my local Woodman pub often centres on country activities, some legal and some not so legal; but only in trusted company. National politics is generally avoided in favour of local issues: potholes, road diversions, flooding, quarry development, field spraying and much else. The true local pub will have a stand out character, The Woodman's latest character, now deceased, was Reg the Waistcoat and also known as Reg the Veg.

Reg's wife, for reasons I never fathomed, kept him supplied with fancy embroidered waistcoats. Reg was always dressed in one of his waistcoats and sometimes I wondered if they were part of his night attire as well – his late wife might have the answer here. His nickname "Reg the Veg" was more obvious because he spend most of his 80+ years on this earth in the local vegetable supply trade. At weekends, he positioned his tractor and trailer full of vegetables at key roadside lay-bys or farm entrances and was never short of customers. Towards the end of his life his vegetables were not always of the highest quality and some well past their sell by date; but it was clear that Reg was going to keep on going to the end and to amuse his customers in his almost now defunct Hertfordshire dialect. There was one extraordinary fact about Reg. He had never been abroad and more surprisingly had never been to London, which is only twenty-five miles from his house near the Woodman pub. Reg might not have been to Germany but the German Luftwaffe came to visit him when he narrowly escaped death from a bomb dropped on Hertford. Not too uncommon for a rural local of Reg's age his reading and writing skills were minimal but he was still capable and forward with interacting with people from all strata of society. Somehow Reg managed to acquire and extend his own home which was a well maintained two storey chalet bungalow in a great location which he left to his only son. A well-paid city professional might just have been able to afford his home. RIP, Reg.

There was a popular Australian song in the 1970s titled "The Pub with no Beer" with lyrics that went —"it's lonesome away from your kindred and all, by the campfire at night where the wild dingoes call, but there is nothing so lonesome, so morbid or drear, than to stand in a bar of a pub with no beer". For me a pub is not just about beer it is about the quality of the beer and above all the quality of its real ale. In the 1970s lager, long since popular in Europe, was becoming ever more popular in Britain. Publicans loved it because it was easy to keep and serve. Pasteurised and served cold with the use of carbon dioxide it could last for weeks in its aluminium or steel kegs. By contrast, real ale was unpasteurised and was served from a mechanical pump at cellar temperature and once the first pint was draw from the barrel it had to be emptied within a few days, otherwise the ale went flat. Real ale is like buying a fresh loaf of bread —best eaten within a day or two otherwise it gets stale. The pipes between the barrel in the cellar and the pump in the bar have to be flushed out daily. Once, when serving in a pub in Norfolk during a hot summer I forgot to flush the pipes and wondered why the customers were not finishing their beer. I checked their beer and found it tasted and smelt like cat's pee. I never made that mistake again. The Campaign for Real Ale, founded in the early 1970s to preserve real ale, has had great success in preserving the real ale tradition. Their advice if you go to a pub with no pumped real ale: drink bottled Guinness or leave. Guinness is a living beer and the fermentation process continues at a greatly reduced level in the sealed bottle. In summer ime, I am partial to German lager mainly because it has no artificial additives under German brewing regulations. A few German beers are top fermented like most British beer and the most famous is Kolsch beer from Cologne.

How a beer is served is important to me. It should have a good head or collar, but not too frothy. Poorly and too quickly poured, the result can look like a pint of milk. I prefer a marked volume glass that leaves room for the correct head size. In the UK such glasses are rare and almost guarantee the publican an extra 10 % profit at the expense of the drinker – disgraceful. Sometimes I like a mug and sometimes a straight glass; but never, never in a plastic container as at football matches. For lager I like the glass to be as thin as possible – it has to be hand washed or you risk breaking it in the dishwasher. Only in Germany have I found glasses of the right thinness. The Belgians are top when it comes to matching glasses to beer types.

Recently craft beers brewed in microbreweries have gained in popularity. Some of them are very good but can be over hopped and expensive. Fermentation is stopped before the bottling process and that is not to the real ale drinker's liking.

There is one type of pub or bar that deserves special mention, namely the Irish pub and it has a unique place in the world of the beer drinker. America has had Irish bars since the mid 19th Century and they are in every city in North America. Britain had a chain of Irish bars in the 19th Century run by JG Mooney from Dublin. The company took over one particularly unique pub, The Boars Head on the Strand in London dating back to 1443, but much changed over the centuries. The pub's present name is "The Tipperary" and I make a point of having a few pints there when in London. The Irish themed pub was a late 20th Century phenomenon and was started by the Irish Pub Company and backed by Guinness. There are now over 7000 Irish themed pubs or bars in 53 countries across the world. Some of the best Irish pubs are in Germany. You can even find Irish pubs in hotels and airports across the world. The O'Reilly chain has pubs even in Russia. When I ran marathons across the world, I always visited an Irish pub not just for Guinness but also for the company.

Unlike in Britain, pubs in Ireland are named after their owners like the famous O'Donohue's Pub – where the Dubliners folk group started out. According to the Guinness Book of Records, the oldest bar in the world is Sean's Bar in Athlone, believed to date from 900AD. I once remember taking my family to Ballyjamesduf in County Cavan the home of the O'Reilly Clan. I expected to find pubs called O'Reilly. Instead, I found pubs called Joe's Bar, Mick's Bar and Paddy's Bar. When I enquired in one bar about this, the publican told me that "sure we would not know who owned which bar if we were all called O'Reillys!. Sure we are all O'Reillys in this town".

May one always have a good waste not want not beer to hand in good company, agus Slainte

ACROSS BORDERS

An tAontas Eorpach
European Union

ÉIRE
IRELAND

Pas
Passport

Your Passport Please

On a pleasant January day my wife and I went to the Norwegian Consular Service in Belgravia, London to renew her passport. All Norwegians living abroad have to present themselves at the Norwegian Embassy or Consular Service in their country of residence to renew or apply for a passport. Dual nationality is not permitted. Ireland does allow dual nationality and does not require attendance at the embassy or consular service in person to renew passports.

My wife had her fingerprints and photo taken and two weeks later received her passport by registered post. The passport contained holographic details that are very difficult to forge.

We then headed for Mayfair and enjoyed a stroll around Grosvenor Square situated in front of the American Embassy. We could not help but note the strict security measures put in place. The current embassy building is deemed to be too small and not secure enough and a new multi-storey cube shaped embassy is due to open south of the Thames in 2017. As we headed deeper into Mayfair we saw a nice pub and it was time for a late morning drink. Whilst I ordered our drinks, Alice got talking to an elderly couple who were waiting for their lunch to arrive. It transpired that the man was a 78-year-old Jordanian and his wife was an English woman from Cheltenham but their main residence was in Amman and they still had a flat in Cheltenham. We told them that we had been to the Norwegian Embassy and when they learned that I had an Irish passport, the husband pulled out from his inside jacket pocket, to my great surprise, his Irish passport.

He came to England in the early 1960s to study Engineering and later got a job with the Jordanian government in weapons procurement. On one of his frequent visits to London, he met his future wife. She told us that her father was from Belfast and had worked in the Harland and Wolf shipyard – no Catholics or Irish nationalist need apply!

Her father was not keen on his daughter converting to Islam to marry her Jordanian boyfriend; but at least he was not a Catholic. She was entitled to an Irish passport because of her father's birthplace and she could retain her UK passport. Her husband was also entitled to an Irish passport by marriage and later on, he acquired one along with his UK and Jordanian passports. It turned out that he had never been to Ireland and that his wife's Irish passport had long since lapsed. However, he believed his Irish passport could be useful in the volatile circumstances of the Middle East.

After the UK voted for Brexit there was a large increase in Irish passport applications. Ireland allows anyone with an Irish born parent or grandparent entitlement to an Irish passport. Applicants were keen to have EU wide travel and work opportunities after Brexit as Ireland would still be an EU member.

I do have some reservations about these "passports of convenience". I can understand why Ireland granted application rights to first and second generation Irish born abroad. The impact of the great 1840s famine and the resultant emigration created a large Irish Diaspora around the world – some 30 million Americans claim Irish descent – and the new Irish Free State, established in 1921, was keen to keep links with the Diaspora who helped to provide economic support for the fledgling state.

As for our Jordanian man, I am not sure what he has ever done for Ireland but I do know that his Irish passport may have a financial and diplomatic commitment from the Irish Government should he use his Irish passport as a refugee or as an enforced captive of any rogue group in the middle east or elsewhere.

Sports people and the rich are two groups that are more favoured when it comes to acquiring passports of convenience. Many countries grant free residence and diplomatic facilities to people who invest a stated minimum amount of money in their country. This can take the form of only buying a house of a defined value. From 2020 rugby players can switch their country of allegiance if they are resident in their second country for 5 years – was 3 years. This elitist approach to granting new nationality is grossly discriminatory towards the poorer would be immigrants and refugees. It calls into question national allegiance and its associated responsibilities. Your passports please!

Do Small Nations have a Purpose or a Future?

Many small countries have to survive on crumbs off the bigger nations' tables but these can sometimes turn into very tasty morsels, like when in June 2016, Iceland beat England in the knockout stage of the European Championship in France and at the same event, Wales got to the semi-final. You could ask why a country with 330,000 inhabitants, straddling the Arctic Circle with no home professional league teams beat a country with over 60 million inhabitants and with the richest premier league in the world. It is true to say that most small countries have no chance of winning the world football cup but they can on occasion get a sensational result against a much bigger country and for that country it is almost like winning a world cup, after all enjoyment is relative. There are sporting events where the smaller country can come in ahead of the big players. Norway topped the Olympic Winter Games gold medal table in 1952, 1968 and in 2018. Jamaica dominating the Olympic sprinting events and Kenya the long distance running events come to mind. New Zealand with only a population of 4.7 million is the exception when it comes to producing a world championship team. By concentrating on rugby union and using the great tradition of the All Blacks, they are the world's number one rugby union team.

What outside of sporting events can a small country achieve? In 2017, the World Happiness Report published by the United Nations placed Norway in first place followed by Denmark, Iceland, Switzerland and Finland. The United States was in 15th, UK 19th, France 31st, Italy 48th and

India 122nd place. The small nations also scored high on per capita income, social support and life expectancy. In passing, the Lonely Planet Blue list 2008 placed Ireland as the world's friendliest country because of its ability to find fun in the best and worst of times.

It was in the 19C that national identity began to come to the fore. The unification of Germany under Bismarck and the unification of Italy under Garibaldi were two primary examples of larger nation creation. Unfortunately, in doing so smaller national identities became subsumed in the process. In the 20C, smaller nations were able to re-establish their independence due to the fall of the German, British, Spanish and the Hapsburg empires. The end of the cold war and the breakup of the Soviet Union allowed a raft of east European countries to reassert themselves, thankfully through peaceful means in most cases. Some small countries had to pay a heavy price for their freedom: Bosnia, Finland (war with Russia 1940s), Ireland and several countries in Africa and South America. The advent of The European Union has given smaller countries for the first time the opportunity to join voluntary an organisation (rather than being coerced into imperial set ups) with the aim of pooling its resources to the benefit of all its members.

Big countries like to exert their control over their minorities within their realm by claiming their actions are in the national interest of unity. In 1949 Mao introduced Beijing time across the country which has a 3000 mile east to west span. India introduced Indian Standard Time for the whole country despite nearly a 2000 mile east to west span. Different time zones can help save energy and tie in more with the local daily work cycle – but national control often takes precedent. In 1916 in the middle of the First World War, the House of Commons in London introduced a bill to bring Irish time (25 minutes behind) into line with English time. Whatever the merits of such a move; the fact that the Irish had lost their own parliament in the Act of Union in 1801, meant that their members were in a numerical minority so the decision would be made by English members in the main.

Many small countries and regions have had great difficulty in preserving their national language. France took measures to suppress Breton and the English Welsh and Irish. Yet a national language is a defining characteristic of a nation's identity. Witness the importance of language in both identity and literature to Norway in its development as a nation. A current example is the struggle between Spanish government and the Catalan Regional government over the status of the Catalan language. The national government knows that reducing the number of Catalan speakers in Catalonia will probably diminish the support for Catalan independence in the longer term.

In science, technology, medicine, art and literature, small nations have made contributions way beyond their size either in their own countries or as immigrants in other countries. One relatively small group of people who have been stateless for nearly 2000 years and who suffered persecution in almost every country they resided in, culminating with the loss of six million in the Holocaust, namely the Jewish Diaspora, have made outstanding achievements across the whole spectrum of human endeavour including: music, film, entertainment, science, medicine, psychology and business.

Ironically, it is the larger countries that have the luxury of telling their subjugated smaller countries that they are too parochial and patriotic and make them the butt of jokes. The English like to ask how many famous Belgians there are? They choose to forget or are ignorant of the fact that Belgium was formed as late as 1831. Belgium is made up of Flemish and French speakers and includes the famous inland historic port of Antwerp home to artists such as: Rubens, Bruegel, van Dyck, Muelen among many other painters. The capital Brussels is also the headquarters of the European Union. Larger countries like to joke about the ignorance or habits of smaller countries and even remote provinces of their own countries.

Samuel Johnson said, "Patriotism was the last refuge of the scoundrel". There is an element of truth in this statement but I think that it applies more to the larger countries in their efforts to expand their territories or empires or in crushing ethnic minorities within their own countries. The independence of the smaller country is a useful foil to stop the formation of the monolithic big country block like the Soviet Union, which under Stalin crushed and eradicated the independence, culture, language and identity of the smaller countries within this block.

Globalisation is viewed by some as a treat to the maintenance of national identities and their culture. Equally, the strengths of the small nations can act as a counter balance.

We can still look forward to maybe another Icelandic football win over say Brazil next time.

The Germans are Coming – FC Koln Invades the Arsenal

I have been an Arsenal fan for many years, inspired by the "Irish Arsenal" Cup winning team of 1979. The team included six Irishmen and an Irish manager and beat Manchester United 3-2. In recent years, the team has acquired a strong French contingent led by a French Manager for 22 years now retired; but within the last few years the team has included a few top German players. Therefore, it came as no surprise to get a text message from Lucas, son of our long-term German friends Mecki and Johannes requesting me to get him European Championship tickets. But it was a big surprise when I realised he wanted tickets for the European Champions Cup match between Spurs v Borussia Dortmund at Wembley Stadium. As an Arsenal fan I immediately let him know that I was not prepared to have any dealings with our local enemy club. Later in the day, he made an alternative request – could I get instead tickets for the Celtic v Munich game in Glasgow. I have a close friend who lives near Glasgow who is a Celtic fan and I replied that I would see what I could do for him. Later in the evening I received another text message pleading if I could get at least 4 tickets for the Europa Cup game between Arsenal and Cologne – the draw had been made a few hours after the European Champions cup draw. Within minutes of his text, I received another text message from Peter, the son of our other long term German friends – Ilse and Hans Peter – begging me for at least 6 tickets for the same match. Peter informed me that the internet was swamped with up to 30000 Cologne fans trying to get tickets for the game. Why this sudden interest from Germany in the game?

Cologne, one of the biggest cities in Germany, has a team that grossly under achieves in the Bundesliga – not unlike our own Newcastle United. They did have some glory days in the 1970s when they had a former Arsenal and England international playing for them, namely Tony Woodcock. Their last appearance in any European competition was 1993 so nearly a quarter of a century on their fans were delighted to have drawn Arsenal and the opportunity to come to London. Unfortunately for European matches, the away fans are only allocated 3000 tickets but despite this 20,000 Cologne fans turned up for the game.

I could get five tickets through family red card membership and the seats would be in the home section. How was I going to hide four big German lads with me from surrounding Arsenal fans? As luck would have it the predominant Cologne team shirt was red like Arsenal. Entry to the ground would not be by ticket but using the red Arsenal membership cards. Instead of Wagners and Mullers they were now all O'Reillys.

I still had the problem of getting six more tickets and had to go online. The ticket sites had barred the sale of any tickets to Cologne supporters, so my six Germans became residents of Hertford and Arsenal supporters. Using my Arsenal member's card, address and UK Master card I was able to convince them we were all British and home fans. I was surprised that I received no normal tickets but six Arsenal red cardholders' passes. My six German friends were now Browns, Crawford and Wades. Clearly, some Arsenal "fans" were making money by loaning their Arsenal red membership cards to the internet ticket sales sites. Understandably, the Germans wanted to be seated together so I had to pay well over £100 per ticket, but such was their desire to be at the match, they were willing to pay the higher ticket prices.

I then heard from my daughter that her boss, a season ticket holder would not be going to the game and he offered his two free hospitality tickets to her. I was not going to turn down such an offer and my German friends now had a spare ticket that they sold to another German. I was now worried that I had two groups of Germans heading for Arsenal supporters enclosures without me to cope with problems that may arise. I made sure that they hid their Cologne fan club gear and at least spoke English as they took their seats – they could pretend to be Norwegians if there were any queries.

We arrived at the Nine Pins Irish pub at Finsbury Park early and after a word with the very relaxed Irish doorkeeper, it was not long before we all had pints of Guinness in our hands. Later my daughter joined us but we were still waiting for Peter to arrive by car from Germany. It transpired that Peter was stuck in traffic and would have to drive straight to the stadium instead of Hertford as previously planned. We all agreed, on our way to the ground, that there was time for another drink at the Auld Triangle Irish pub. After a bit of a chat with the door attendant I got all my new "Arsenal Norwegian" fans into this staunch home fan pub. As we were well into our pints of Guinness a newsflash appeared on the pub TV – "Start of match delayed until 9pm – one hour". Seemingly, some of the 20000 Cologne fans had stormed the entrance gate – a lot of them gaining entry.

Still no sign of Peter and his friend; but time for another pint. As we were well into our second pint Peter and friend arrived in time for at least a quick pint – if the match had not been delayed for an hour he would have missed the game as we had his tickets.

As we headed up towards the stadium, there were very few fans around – all in the stadium by now - and we went our separate ways to get in.

The match started in a relatively subdued atmosphere and after about 20 minutes Cologne scored and one end of the stadium erupted, fireworks going off and it seemed as if they were about 15000 Cologne fans in the stadium instead of the allotted 3000. They had shown amazing ingenuity in getting tickets and getting in without tickets. A quiet second half followed a very raucous first half as Arsenal scored three unanswered goals to win the match.

Even though they lost, the Cologne fans stayed on in the stadium after the match to celebrate their moment in the limelight. It was midnight before my friends joined me for a final pint of Guinness in the Nine Pins.

Next day my wife Alice made them a big brunch and they headed home in good spirits. As for me, I was left to enjoy all the Kolsch German beer they had brought with them. Prost.

TWO WHEELS
BETTER THAN ONE

On Yer Bikes – 2
Wheels Better than 4

"Every time I see an adult on a bicycle, I no longer despair for the future of the human race" H G WELLS

The invention of the wheel and all devices associated with it gave man the opportunity to explore the world way beyond his immediate environment. But it was not until the late 19th Century with the invention of the chain driven two wheel bike with its pneumatic tyres gave local people the opportunity to cycle many miles beyond their own villages and meet the new love of their lives, which in turn strengthened the human gene pool.

As we proceed through the early part of the 21st century cycling has regained the widespread use and excitement that it gained during the early part of the 20th century. Even the penny-farthing is gaining a keen fan club. Cycling was set free from its "bone shaker" beginnings by the invention the chain-gear system and the pneumatic tyre that allowed for smaller wheels and a safer smoother ride. Surprising the basic triangular frame shape has not changed much over the years; but there has been a big leap forwards in weight reduction – carbon frames – and in braking systems that include disc brakes. In the 1970s, a whole new range of mountain and off- road bikes were developed in California and many companies continue to create even more exotic bikes - I have a cousin who bikes down ski slopes on a bike with enormous tyres – something for me to look forward to trying in the future.

I learned to ride a bike in rural Ireland in the 1950s. We had to learn to ride on adult bikes. Kids did not get bicycles as Christmas or birthday presents back then, although I did see the odd townie rich kid on a tricycle now and then. I learned to cycle using my grandmother's bike and being small of stature had to ride standing up on the pedals as the saddle was too high for me. I then progressed to riding a man's bike by holding by right arm over the saddle and steering with my left hand whilst squeezed under the cross bar. I even managed to break whilst in this contorted position but I was not always successful and ended up with many bruises and scratches when I fell off. Neighbouring kids were a source of inspiration in finding new ways to ride our adult bikes. I learned to sit on the carry rack behind the saddle and steer the bike with fully stretched arms using the tips of my fingers. Breaking was not an option in this position. When I was about twelve, I progressed to using the bike as a taxi for the smaller of the neighbouring kids. The ultimate achievement was to have one kid balanced on the handlebars, one on the crossbar and one on the carriage behind the saddle. It was a bit easier to achieve this with my grandmother's bike by riding standing up with the third kid sitting on the saddle. In time, nearly all the local kids could ride bikes without using the handlebars. Today the modern lightweight design of children's bikes allows them to do 'wheelies' and other tricks.

When I moved to London in 1960, the bus and tube became my main mode of transport as well as walking. I did buy an old bike from an acquaintance – probably stolen! – and cycled from Swiss Cottage to Camden Town and on past the Royal Holloway women's prison to visit my grandmother who lived in Haringey some eight miles away. There were not many people on bikes in London then and I was lucky to survive the journey with no safety equipment and little experience of the congested and polluting London traffic. Even now, it scares me to think of the smoke belching from the Double- Decker London buses passing within inches of me. My second memorable London bike ride was a strike for the open countryside and the cows that I missed since leaving Ireland. After cycling from Finchley to Golders Green and on towards Barnet I struck lucky when I saw some cows in a field surrounded by blocks of flats on two sides. I thought it strange to see cows in what was still a semi- urban environment. Even better was the discovery of a milk dispensing machine. Refreshed by a cold carton of milk I had time to greet my new four legged friends and then head back the 10 miles or so home very satisfied with my trip to the "countryside". It was only later that I found out that this small farm was a research dairy centre and I was still some miles away from the open Hertfordshire countryside to the north of London.

It was nearly twenty years – 1980- before I reacquainted myself with cycling. This time I bought a second hand racing bike to ride on occasions the 20 mile round trip to my school in Hertfordshire. I was safety conscientious enough to wear an old-fashioned grid felt strapped headgear – the modern moulded helmet had not yet seen the light of day. I added a few reflectors and a protruding side reflector to stop the cars and Lorries getting too near to me. Sometimes I used a peddle foot strap to give extra back lift – the modern cleats had still to make an appearance. These could be quite dangerous if you did not get your foot out in time when breaking and coming to a stop. The ride to school was on small country roads with a couple of testing hills and there were times when I was able to collect a few relatively undamaged pheasants killed by the odd car. There was one cyclist, who passed me nearly every morning on his way to London Bridge some thirty miles from his home. He cycled all year round and I can only admire his resilience especially having to ride all the way back after a day at work. He did this journey in the early 1980s and was way ahead of his time. When it snowed heavily overnight, I was often the first teacher to get to work. One had no problem in cycling through the soft snow; in fact, it was an exuberating experience. It was only later when the snow was churned up by traffic, then frozen overnight that the cycling got tough.

When I moved school in 1988, the journey there was nearly 30 miles and on main roads, so cycling was out of the question. However I did buy myself a vintage Rayleigh 531 racing frame bike in good condition which I used now and again for a ride round my local countryside.

My cycling got a boost when I received a lightweight Norwegian straight handle bar Everest bike for my 60th birthday. This bike had the gear changing mechanism as part of the steering bars, a great step forward in bicycle design. Unfortunately the bike was stolen from outside my Gym a few months later but I got an identical replacement from my insurance company. It was not long before I wanted an out and out racer and duly purchased one from Wiggle.com, a Felt out of season bike for £1650 weighing in at an impressive 7.2 Kg. It took me some time to get used to using cleats but I soon appreciated the extra bike control and increase in pedal power on hill climbing. Whilst caravanning in the south of France in 2014 I met a German who was a keen club cyclist and he took me to a new level. He guided me on a 90km bike ride in the hills overlooking the San Tropez peninsula. I learnt to climb steady for nearly an hour up winding hill climbs in the lowest gear, but I could not match his downhill speeds. He told me there are three rules for going downhill: do not break, if you have to use only your front break and lean into the bends. I still have not quite mastered these skills to my satisfaction.

My youngest son is a keen cyclist and he could not resist borrowing my Felt for his London to Brussels 24-hour bike ride and his London to Brighton ride. I cannot remember if he borrowed my bike for his Liverpool to London charity ride but I ended up letting him keep the Felt and my Everest. I was not long bikeless and treated myself to a Bianchi Italian job weighing in at 7.5Kg. My son did teach me the value of cadence, bike geometry, tyre pressure, saddle height and using energy gels on longer bike rides. He has since acquired for himself a racing bike that suits his body size and style of racing but at a price.

My greatest achievement to date was participating in the London-Surrey 100 mile Olympic Legacy sportive with my son in aid of Cystic Fibrosis in 2015. I was lucky to get an early start and avoid a pile up on the category 2 Leith Hill to finish in just under 6 hours plus 10 minutes for refreshment stops. My previous marathon running experience was a great help not to mention those energy gels.

Time to get on my bike.

Marathon Bike Ride

I have been involved in marathon running and charity fund raising adventures across the world since 1984. Little did I realise that at the age of 69 I would undertake a different type of marathon activity – **The Prudential 100 Mile Olympic Legacy London-Surrey Sportive Bike Ride.**

On a beautiful sunny early morning on August 2nd 2015, my son and I lined up with 35000 other cyclists in the Olympic Queen Elizabeth 2nd Park, London and just less than six hours later I rode down The Mall to the finish in front of Buckingham Palace.

I have cycled over the years as a means of getting to school and later to work or on holiday, but never in a competitive race. I did get a present of a light carbon framed bike for my 60th birthday but my son had already got the cycle bug and borrowed it – permanently. However impressed by his London to Brussels and London to Paris bike rides I bought myself another carbon framed racing bike in the hope that I might join the action. The former Mayor of London and now Prime Minister Boris Johnson's efforts to promote cycling also encouraged me to get back on my bike. Once he turned up on his bike at the City of London Girls' School when I taught there to give a talk to the girls. I ignored the bit of his talk when he said he was not a great fan of regulations and never wore a cycle helmet.

Unfortunately, I was rejected two years running in the entry ballot for the Prudential 100 Mile — one would have thought that a 68 year old had a good chance of gaining entry as a senior. Entries were still available through the many charities participating in the event. The charity Cystic Fibrosis (CF) gave entries to my son and me with the proviso that we raise £1500 for them.

My vibrant lovely then 13-year old granddaughter drew the genetic short straw in the ballot of life. She had an open-heart operation as a four-month old baby in The Royal Brompton, London that may have weakened her lungs leading to the development of a disease that mimics Cystic Fibrosis. She also suffers from celiac. The decision to support CF was an easy one to make for my son and me.

The major difference between a bike race and a marathon run is that you have to look after the bike as well as yourself. Will I get a puncture? Will the chain snap? Will unseen potholes buckle the wheels? Will I skid on loose gravel on the road? Will I collide with other riders? Do I have my clothing, energy supply and safety correct for this marathon ride?

Marathon running requires one to get some long and testing training sessions done well before the event. Marathon bike riding is no different. I managed several bike rides of 25, 30, 40 miles and a few at 50 and 70 miles in all sorts of weather. In Hertfordshire, we are lucky to have some challenging hills and it is as important to be able to descend as well as ascend.

It was a very early rise of 4.30am on race day for a 7.15 start. The elite riders started at 6.00am. My wife dropped us off about five miles from the Olympic Park – roads closed to traffic – and we cycled the rest of the way. Time for a strong coffee, check the tyre pressure, toilet stop and then join the correct channel for my start time. My son had a later start time.

The ride along the A12 dual carriageway in wonderful sunshine, free of traffic, towards Canary Wharf was exhilarating and I reached 30mph with little effort. The previous year the weather was so bad that the race organisers reduced the distance to avoid accidents and exposure.

Soon Canary Wharf was behind us and I could see the new Shard tower, the highest building in Europe, in the distance. The streets were still spectator free except for the last of the all night clubbers and some keen early morning tourists. We sped past the Tower of London, a familiar sight from many of my London marathon runs, and on past St Paul's Cathedral and down Fleet Street towards Piccadilly Circus. Then pass Harrods, no time or money for shopping and on to Chiswick and Richmond Park.The Park was much larger than I expected and included our first real hill climb. There were now more spectators, especially as we went through Kingston upon Thames and towards the Surrey Hills. We had three category 2 Tour de France climbs ahead. The first after 48 miles was Newlands Corner that I managed well. The real test came at 55 miles, Leith Hill the highest point in the South East of England. I realised the going was tough when I passed many cyclist who were walking, but I kept going in my lowest gear until about 100 yards from the top where I was completely blinded by sweat running into my eyes. At the top, I sorted out my energy gels and I had a good wodge of kitchen towel paper to absorb the excess sweat and got going again. The next challenge was Box Hill at 70 miles and I was ready for it. It turned out to be manageable because it had a few hairpin bends that Leith Hill did not have. One more stop for a water refill and I was on my way to the finish coming down off the North Downs to climb two more hills at Kingston and Wimbledon. We cycled over Putney Bridge and then hit the home stretch through Hammersmith and Chelsea. I managed the last 20 miles to The Mall in 55 minutes that gave me an average speed of over 20mph.

My son who started in a later wave was unfortunately held up at the bottom of Leith Hill when the air ambulance landed to deal with a collapsed rider who sadly died. He was worried that it might have been me - 3 years since my heart bypass - but was relieved to see that the dead rider's abandoned bike was not mine. He went on to finish the rest of the ride in a good time.

When I reached the finish, I was pleased to see my wife, daughter and especially my granddaughter with a lovely smile on her face. I think she was delighted and relieved that I completed the ride and even more so knowing that her dad and we had collected well over £2000 for Cystic Fibrosis - the real winner on the day.

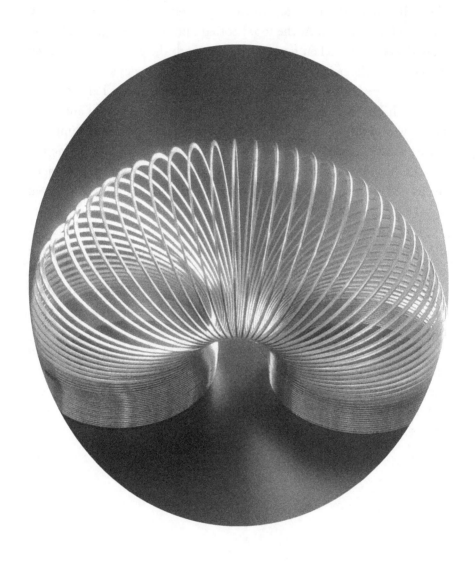

Springs ~ All Sorts

Springs as a subject of scientific interest can be a rewarding pursuit; but as a means to become a billionaire might not readily spring to mind. Springs in all their shapes and sizes have been fundamental to the workings of the many mechanisms and concepts that drive our modern world.

I had not realised how making springs could help one to become a billionaire until I met a Chinese student at one of the private schools where I though Physics. His English was very basic but he did have a good understanding of the language of Mathematics. One day I happened to ask him what his father back in China worked at. He gave a one-word answer - "springs" in a heavy Chinese accent. I asked him what kind of springs he manufactured. "All sorts", he replied. It was then that I realised that his father must be very rich. When pressed as to what type of springs, he said all sorts of springs for aircraft, trains, watches, cars, lifts, buildings.

The most familiar spring is the helical that school children use to demonstrate Hook's Law that the extension is directly proportion to the force of extension or compression as long as you keep within the elastic limit, beyond which the spring will not return to its original length. For a small sum one can buy a slinky spring and have fun walking it down stairs, setting up transverse and or longitudinal waves as well as standing waves like those in a church organ. However, there is not much money to be made from these small springs. You need to go much smaller or bigger and produce large quantities. Most people have a dress watch and the lucky ones have a watch in the Rolex class. These watches contain many delicate coil springs that are manufactured by the million.

There are millions of cars in the world and most of these need large robust shock-absorbing springs and hydraulic piston springs. There are millions of cars in China and beyond so making only a fraction of these springs can make one very rich. The boom in air traffic means more planes along with the vital and expensive shock absorbing spring landing gear. China has a large military and every gun needs a recoil mechanism – millions of guns needed.

In everyday life, we depend on the use of mechanisms that involve springs from hairpins, bicycle clips, ski boots, paper clips and much more.

Wherever you have vibrations you have the spring effect. Your own body can be a great percussion drum from your head to your back to your stomach and doctors just love to tap us to hear those vibrations. At the atomic level, we imagine little springs attaching atom to atom and they can vibrate at very high frequencies. We now have caesium atom clocks that only lose about 1 second in 30 million years and are used to control and synchronise GPS systems. I do not know if our Chinese student's dad is into atomic clocks but it could be another opportunity for him to diversify the business.

Latest research in neurology is making a case that brain information may be transmitted by tiny mechanical vibrations as well as the traditional electrical signal transmissions.

China has been on a building frenzy for decades and some of its cities are now on a par with New York when it comes to the number of skyscrapers. A tall building is a bit like a diving board that oscillates at the top and like diving boards need damping mechanism to stop resonance to protect the building from collapse and reduce swaying to prevent sickness in the workers. Large costly oscillating pendulum like mechanism are built to counteract the natural oscillations of the building. The same applies to bridges and everybody knows about the wobbly London millennium bridge which cost a lot of money to correct resulting in closing the bridge after its brief opening in 2000. Unusually the problem was due to lateral sway caused by the pedestrians amplifying the motion of the bridge by instinctively being in step with the small sway to start with and ends up causing resonance.

I noticed my Chinese student left the lab with an extra spring in his step in the knowledge of his inherited riches to come. As for me, I left the lab for morning coffee and to reflect on how, despite my knowledge of springs, failed to take off in making my fortune.

LIFE'S SURPRISES

Silly Billy the Cat – Enters our Lives

"Cats are great connoisseurs of comfort"- James Herriot

There may be up to eight million cats and nine million dogs in Britain but our cat Silly Billy was for us really one in a million.

Our two sons, more than a decade older than their sister Astrid had left home, so it was time for a member of the small animal world to occupy the space vacated in our house. Enter two Gerbils – Midi and Sunny, black and dark furred respectively. Such was our daughter's delight with our nocturnal manic new friends she soon started to agitate for an extension to her menagerie, namely a cat.

We applied to a local cat refuge centre in Hertfordshire and were surprised that they insisted that we must first be interviewed as to our suitability to be a responsible cat owner. The woman interviewer was white middle class with a sense of her own importance. Despite having a detached house with secluded front and back gardens and my early childhood farm experience, we received a letter rejecting our application. I am not sure the two manic Gerbils helped our case. But we were not easily deterred. We visited a refuge centre for abandoned cats in Harlow – a step down the social ladder from the one in Hertfordshire but far more in touch with the real world of pet ownership. We were spoilt for choice; but two cats caught our eye – one a largish all black very friendly cat and one much smaller, very shy and with beautiful black and white markings. We opted with some misgivings for the latter. Armed with our new cat cage, bedding and cat feed we brought a very reluctant cat home with us. We let him free in the lounge only to find that he immediately hid under a sideboard and would not come out. It took us several days to entice him to come out to feed without having to put the food underneath the sideboard or armchair. His odd behaviour enticed my wife to coin the name "Silly Billy".

Silly Billy soon started to grow and become quite aggressive. He did not like it when we tried to pick him up for a cuddle and we risked being caught by a swinging claw or gnashing teeth. For Silly Billy it was not love at first sight but we grew to like his aggressive antics and his independence. We had him neutered and that made him a little less aggressive.

We thought that Silly Billy would grow quickly but he remained relatively small for a male cat. He was quite capable of defending his territory against much bigger neighbouring Tomcats. We were also disappointed with his mouse catching ability and I can only remember Billy catching one mouse in the kitchen when my wife opened a cupboard door and Billy caught the mouse in midair as it tried to jump to freedom. My wife was very impressed and thereafter was always willing to sing Billy's skills as a mouse catcher. He did once bring home a mouse to our front door.

Early on I started to pick Billy up by the loose fur skin on the back of his neck as mother cats sometimes do with their own young. This allowed me to show Billy that I could be the boss at least some of the time and he always remained very still until I put him down again. Slowly, but surely, he would stay on my daughter's and my lap only if covered with a blanket or cushion. Billy liked his comforts. He would often prefer to lie on top of a cushion on the settee rather than the settee itself. Eventually it got to the stage that after his breakfast Billy would lie flat-out belly up on my outstretched legs and I could stroke his belly; but the decision to do so was always his.

The time came when we had to take him to the cattery and Billy hated it. Sometimes he would sense that I was getting his cage and he would do a runner. He would meow in the car all the way to the cattery. Astrid and I felt very sad about this and it was all the more painful because other cats there did not seem to mind their temporary incarceration. When we went to collect him I could hear him meowing as soon as he heard our voices and continued all the way back until we released into the garden and there he ran around too excited to eat the tasty morsels we put out for him. Having said that, the cattery we got for him was local and had an individual open-air enclosure for Billy to move around in and experience the sounds and smells of the surrounding woodlands. It was the most expensive in Hertfordshire but still unappreciated by Billy. Silly Billy was five years old when Astrid left home on a gap year and then university. The sad task of taking and collecting Billy from the cattery was now mainly mine.

When we went out Billy's favourite position was a spot underneath our front privet hedge from which he would emerge before our car got to the drive having learnt to recognise the sound of our Honda motor. On many occasions on my way home from the pub Billy would recognise the sound of my footsteps. He would come out on to the roadside pavement and roll around on his back to welcome me home. He would then dart towards the hall door knowing he was going to be rewarded with a late supper snack. As I drank my nightcap listening to music, Billy would be happy to lay stretched out on my lap – that is until the smell of alcohol overcame him and then even I realised it was time for me to go to bed.

At Christmas Billy would seek out even more comfortable positions to lie on than his usual cushions. Under our Christmas tree in the conservatory with heated tiled floor was his favourite spot. As we got closer to Christmas Day, more presents were placed under the tree and Billy resorted to finding the softest paper wrapped present to lie on. I will never forget one Christmas day, when our family arrived for the present opening only to find Bill stretched out on top of his favourite wrapped present under the Christmas tree. He was not at all happy to see his favourite lie on presents removed one by one – but he still stayed under the tree during all the noise and excitement as the grandchildren "ripped open" their presents. Our grandchildren felt that Billy only "liked me" – not surprising as some of them bore some of Billy's scratch marks and even the odd bite mark.

It is surprising how much a cat and its living habits can impact on one's daily life. In 2012 I had a heart bypass and was in hospital for eight days. I was surprised how much I missed Billy despite my own travails and I was delighted to see him again when I got home.

The final years.

As Billy got older, he became more house bound. I remember opening the front door for him as he indicated that he wanted to go out. It was windy and rainy outside but not too cold. Billy advanced took a few sniffs of air and darted back into the lounge and onto his favourite chair. As ever, he hated even more the idea of going to the cattery. He grew thinner and a little bonier but still looked great in his black and white markings.

In March 2013 when Billy was 14 years old, my wife and I went on an eight-day Mediterranean cruise that included visits to the Egyptian Pyramids and Israel. I failed to get him a place in the local cattery and took him to a cattery a few miles away where he had been before. He was a little off his food and I told the cattery owner to keep an eye on him and take him to a vet if necessary.

My wife and I enjoyed floating in the Dead Sea and the fun in trying to do a breaststroke swim with one's posterior sticking out of the water. Later in the day we took a cable car up to the top of Masada overlooking the Dead Sea. Masada is the place where it is said that a besieged group of Jews committed an organised collective suicide to save them from capture and slavery by the attacking Roman army. As I walked around this sparse and exposed hillside fort, I received a mobile call. To my surprise it was the lady from the cattery. Billy had died in her arms that morning. She had wrapped him in a blanket and put him in a fridge. My wife and I were upset about poor Billy's demise and Masada took on a new meaning for us.

My daughter Astrid and I buried Billy in his favourite place under the privet hedge on our front drive. Even now some years on from Billy's death we still expect to see him coming out from under the hedge to greet us. Thank you, Billy, for the memories and for being part of our lives.

...LEAR FISSION of URA...

$$^{235}_{92}M + ^{1}_{0}n \rightarrow ^{141}_{56}Ba + ^{92}_{36}Kr + 3...$$

NUCLEAR FUSION of HELIUM

$$^{4}_{2}He + ^{4}_{2}He \rightarrow ^{8}_{4}Be$$

THEN $$^{4}_{2}He + ^{8}_{4}Be \rightarrow ^{12}_{6}C + 2\gamma$$

Making a Difference

We all live in societies that depend on human cooperation and endeavour for our prosperity and happiness. Everyone's contribution, small or big, matters. I make no claim that my contribution is more valuable than those of my fellow citizens. I hope that, given the opportunities that society has afforded me, that I have made a difference to the progress and future prospects of my students in my years as a teacher.

I had the opportunity to take early retirement at the age of 54 in 1999 and I gladly grasped it with both hands. I thought rightly or wrongly, that after over 30 years of continuous teaching I had made a significant contribution to the education of young people. Little did I realise that taking on teaching contracts post retirement in some of England's elite private schools would require me to make a difference to the education of young people on a par with anything that I may have achieved in the past as a full-time teacher in the state sector.

My first experience of education in England was when I left Ireland in 1960 at the age of 14. I had a happy experience at my local secondary modern school in Kentish Town, London. I managed to do well at GCE O' and A' levels and started a Physics degree at Queen Mary College, London University. Incidentally, a new Labour government closed down my school in 1997 because it was judged to be underperforming.

My university experiences included various jobs to help pay living costs and a term as President of the London University Debating Society that allowed me to experience some student life at other universities.

I started my teaching career at Finchley Catholic Boys' Grammar School – the first time that I set foot in a grammar school. Later I got a post as Head of Physics at Burnham Grammar School - still in existence.

By now, the early 1970s, the comprehensive movement was taking root and I desperately wanted to be part of it.

As Head of Science at a comprehensive school in Maidenhead, I had the opportunity to be involved in establishing new laboratories and appropriate Nuffield inspired curricula, based on pupil designed science experiments, for the new generation of comprehensive schools.

Deputy Headship in Hertfordshire from 1980 to 1999 provided a different set of challenges. Falling school rolls involved me in first a school amalgamation and later a school closure resulting in redeployment. I gained valuable experience and enjoyment supporting pupils and staff in very trying circumstances.

My efforts to get interviews for headships in the shire counties were not very successful. My prospects were not enhanced by the reaction of governing bodies to the activities of the IRA and my own republican Irish background coupled to some historical anti-Catholicism. One helpful LEA Education Officer even suggested that I might be better off going back to the Catholic sector and then trying for headships in inner city areas. Nevertheless, I finished my career with a very rewarding 11 years as Deputy Head Master of Ashlyns Upper School (formerly The Thomas Coram Foundling Hospital of London) in Berkhamstead, Herts. It is amazing to think how attitudes towards the Irish have changed for the better in recent years.

I have to admit that I was jaded by all the implications resulting from endless political initiatives of the 1990s - was it that the loss of Empire freed up a lot of civil servants to impose their rules and paperwork on the beleaguered education, health service and other public sectors? The prospect of staying in the same school as deputy to retirement at sixty was not a very challenging one but more a long-term prospect of seeing your time out.

My passion for direct 'real teaching and learning' had to take a back seat during my 20 years as a deputy head. I had never lost my interest in science and love of learning. Changes in Grant Maintained Status gave me the opportunity to retire early in 1999 and a chance to get back into the classroom and laboratory.

My first contract was for one term when I helped a colleague in a tough school and this got me back into the rhythm of classroom teaching and survival. An opportunity then arose to teach Mathematics at Mill Hill Public School, London to cover a maternity leave. This was my first introduction to the private sector and Saturday teaching! The experience was challenging, rewarding and enjoyable. My years in the state sector were a great help in coping with the surprising amount of responsibility that the management delegated to me, including roles in the sporting and cultural life of the school. However, it was the shock of teaching four one-hour long lessons on the Saturday, which made the biggest impact on me – no more Friday nights in my local pub. Teaching mathematics to a very tired lower band group early Saturday afternoon was a particular challenge to me but even more so to the students.

I still have flashbacks of my responsibly for junior cross country runs in the winter twilight months when there were times when I lost some of the pupils in the increasing darkness or others came to grief on the icy lanes in the challenging hills and forest around Mill Hill.

My next post was to teach Physics at The City of London School for Girls. The new Head of Physics could not take up his appointment until the following term. The school is located at the centre of the London Barbican and imbibes some of dynamism that is part of the City of London. Needless to say the girls and staff were wonderful and I felt that my services were valued and appreciated. At that time the school was in top position in the national school performance table, well ahead of Eton and other more ancient established public schools. I was to return to this school again in 2007 for an even more rewarding experience.

Illness can strike down a teacher at any time and lead to an emergency replacement being required. Sadly, this was the reason why I took over a valued and experienced member of staff's timetable at Alleyns School, Dulwich in mid- January 2002. It can be difficult to step into the shoes of a popular and outstanding teacher; but this was one of my strengths. It was the main reason why I commanded a relatively high salary. The commute from Hertford to South London using two main railway lines plus underground was a challenge in itself, made easier by a timely coffee on the way at London Bridge. I have always believed that the travel time is worth it when your services are appreciated by the pupils. In fact, the school asked me to take on a second contract after the ill colleague returned because of other staff issues.

To make a real impact in a school it is important to contribute to school life beyond the classroom. My interest in marathon running and fund raising was useful here. Since my first London marathon in 1984, I have managed to run two or three marathons a year. To date I have run marathons in 30 countries including most of the big city marathons. A very important part of this hobby of mine is the opportunity that it affords to meet people and engage the young people that I teach in sponsoring various charities. I have pleasant memories of running the Budapest marathon on behalf of Alleyns School nominated charity - The Delmaza House Hospice for Children.

After a short break I returned to the state sector and took a contract at short notice at The Coopers and Coburn School, Upminster. This is one of the top mixed comprehensive schools in the country. This time I had a 40 mile commute using the A10 and M25. I can remember dismissing my class 5 minutes early to make a quick getaway as I saw the first snowflakes falling one winter's day. That decision meant that I just missed the ensuing gridlock on the M25 and M11 that involved commuters stranded in their cars overnight. I have also fond memories of the rugby team reaching the schools' rugby final at Twickenham and a small year 7 boy running 14 miles round the sports field with me as part of the school's charity fund raising day. I ended up taking a second contract at this school and was pleased to be able to again engage my marathon hobby by giving assembles in support of running the Prague marathon in aid of the school's nominated charity - The St Francis Hospice.

My biggest and one of the most challenging contracts was still to come – a one-year full-time post at St Paul's School for Girls (SPGS), London.

SPGS was officially opened in 1904 by Princess Mary and HRH George, Prince of Wales. It was founded for the education of elite girls to instil a sense of independence and an ethos based on 'everything is possible'. In 1905 a certain Gustav Holst was appointed Director of Music and listed in the staff handbook under 'Assistant Mistresses'. In the century that followed, Paulinas have made a great contribution towards advancing women's education and their role in society.

I was only thinking of a short part-time contract but ended up as a full-time teacher – the only one in the Physics department of four staff and an assistant form tutor as well. Despite my considerable previous experience, I still struggled to win some of the girls over in the early stages. Questions, questions and more questions were the order of the day. Often lessons took a turn into areas of scientific knowledge that went well beyond the scheme of work. If a girl got 98% in a test, you had to be ready to explain why she did not get 100%. The school has never had a school uniform as such and this reflects the independence of mind and individuality of the girls. I remember asking a class to organise their own Christmas quiz - a simple task you might think. I ended up doing it myself. As one of the girls told me, 'we are all too self- opinionated to agree to anything'.

It was wonderful to be part of a very creative and gifted student environment. I felt that I was making a difference. Beyond the classroom I was able to organise a joint school assembly with selected girls on the history of women's marathon running linked to my own experiences of running marathons over 25 years. Appropriately, for such a musically gifted school I ran the 250th Mozart Birthday Vienna Marathon in support of the girl's nominated charity. I also have fond memories of staff talent shows and the various extra-curricular activities put on by the girls.

In June 2006 I reached the age of 60 years and thought that finishing my teaching career at SPGS would be a good time to call it a day.

Soon afterwards, a businessperson friend of mine talked about the need to make a difference in life. I thought that maybe I should do some voluntary work abroad. On second thoughts, I came to the conclusions that other people could do a better job than me. I still knew that the future leaders of this country needed to be inspired by high quality teaching and learning. My experiences in education I felt equipped me well- rightly or wrongly - to do this. Yes, I felt I still could make a difference. So a bit like Frank Sinatra, I could not resist coming back one more time.

Once again The City of London Girls needed someone to take a post pending the arrival of a new head of department. Even in top schools students for various reasons may at times not be able to receive the quality of teaching they deserve and that their parents paid for. My task was to restore confidence and raise standards with some classes deemed to have missed out and do it quickly. I was amazed how well the girls responded. I was even more impressed by the positive response from their parents. A very good working relationship with the Physics technician was key to delivering the scheme of work. It was not long before I got to give a couple of assemblies on my favourite subject and this resulted in my running the Duchy of Cornwell Marathon on a very windy, cold but sunny March Sunday on behalf of the school's elected charity. But sadly my stay had to come to an end and it was extremely hard to leave the girls and staff. I think some of the girls felt let down. I felt it very difficult to leave and somewhat emotional. I thought that age and experience would have hardened me to departures. Surprisingly pupils can become attached to teachers and do not like change. However I believed that I had made a real difference - mission accomplished.

In late November 2007, I decided to rejoin the teaching fraternity. This time I went back to my roots - a very popular inner city comprehensive - Camden School for Girls with a very large mixed sixth form. This school is less than a mile from the closed down school that I was a pupil in when I first came to London out of Ireland.

This time I did not make a difference and resigned after only three weeks. I had to share lessons with another temporary teacher, lack of resources, poor timetabling- nearly 2 hour lessons for younger pupils and contrary to all research recommendations. Above all, there was an extraordinary entitlement and expectation from some recent immigrant pupils. This probably came from over pampering from staff and Governors to their immigrant, religious and in some cases, refugee background and in my view was at the expense of the indigenous pupil. On one occasion, I called the Head teacher to come to one of my classes and in front of her and the pupils gave a lecture to all on how privileged and humble I was as an Irish immigrant to get a free education, including free milk and books. As an immigrant, I did not come with entitlement or expect that the country owed me a living. I think they got the message and maybe I did make a difference in changing the attitudes of a few immigrant girls in this particular class and even more important that of the Head teacher. However, it was too little too late and this school is the only one that I felt that I had failed.

Soon another and wonderful opportunity came for me to join the staff of St Edmund's College, England's oldest Catholic School. This was to be my swansong.

The first school that I taught in was Finchley Catholic Boys Grammar

School, but it was to be nearly 40 years before my return to a catholic school. Upon reflection my career path and associated promotion would have been a lot easier if I had stayed but I preferred the more challenging semi secular state system of education, even if at times some of its inbuilt anti Irish and anti Catholic undercurrents, particular prevalent in school Governing Bodies, was not always to my advantage.

St Edmunds was for many years a catholic seminary and for a long period had to be relocated to Douai, France and only returned to England after Catholic Emancipation in 1829.The College had a new lease of life and were able to build a fine Pugin designed Chapel. My daughter had been Head Girl at the school in 2003 and this proved to be an added attraction for me.

The school needed someone as a matter of some urgency to take over for the head of physics. Fee paying parents rightly are not too happy when their children have no experienced physics GCE A 'Level teacher a matter of only months before their public examination. These are just the circumstances where I can hit the ground running and make an immediate difference. Yes hard work for me, but a joy when one is appreciated by the students and parents.

Maybe I could have been successful in some other occupation, but it is difficult to surpass the joy of teaching and guiding young people at a key stage in their life's journey. Everybody remembers the teacher that made a difference.

A Chance Encounter

Over the years there have been special occasions when I have been fortunate to meet by chance people who have revealed to me an unexpected, intimate and heartfelt event that happened in their life. With time my memory of these chance encounters has faded and in retrospect I wish I had recorded the encounter for future reflection. In the main, the encounters were life enhancing and restored my faith in the intrinsic goodness of people that transcends national, religious and other human traits that can divide us. The following recent encounter is a typical example.

Sunday 11th November 2018 was a beautiful pleasant sunny day and the opportunity for a walk rather than drive into town was not to be missed, especially as I had to purchase a chicken for a late roast dinner. The day was also special as it was 100 years since the end of the Great War and there were still medal-bedecked veterans milling around the town centre after their Remembrance Day parade.

On the way home I strolled through a small open garden of tranquillity, recently created by a local stalwart, when I encountered a solitary tall, slim elderly man admiring the shrubs and surroundings. Circumstances were such that a brief greeting would not suffice so I asked him if he were a visitor to the area and he replied that he was a local, but originally came from East London where he was born before World War 2. He looked much younger and fitter than his four score years. His father had moved the family out of London after their house was destroyed in a German bombing raid – they got to the bomb shelter in time.

He completed an apprenticeship and became a local tradesman in the building industry. I complimented him on his fitness but over the years I have come to realise that nearly everybody over the age of fifty has a personal health story and his was that he had a severe heart attack caused by a blood clot at the age of 59 years but survived to tell the tale. Upon hearing that I was Irish, he told me of his wonderful Irish grandfather, not too surprising as about six million English people are entitled to claim an Irish passport due to having at least one Irish grandparent. He then revealed that he had an only son and I could see that he was becoming a bit emotional. Four years previously, he had received a phone call from his son who had been taken by emergency ambulance to hospital. His son told him to come as soon as possible but he would not say what was wrong with him until he arrived at the hospital. By now the tears were welling up in his eyes when he told me that upon arrival at the hospital he was directed to the intensive care department. I was now expecting the worst. His then 48-year-old son told him that he had only months to live – he had a complete lung malfunction and the only hope of saving his life was to have a lung transplant. He told the consultant there and then that he wanted his son to have one of his lungs. Unfortunately he turned out not to be a suitable donor but a few weeks later suitable donor lungs were taken from a young women killed in a car crash near Newcastle. His son was transferred to Newcastle University Hospital where he had a successful transplant. The months and years after the transplant were not easy for his son, his family or his father. He told me how painful as a father it was to watch his former very fit son struggling to walk a few steps connected to all sorts of medical equipment but at least he had survived.

I confided in him my own health trials and tribulations but they paled into insignificance to those of his son. I do not know how long we were in conversation because the two of us were oblivious to our surroundings, locked together in a powerful grasp of emotional togetherness. Then slowly the sunlit shrubs came back into focus, his tears had dried up and we parted to go back into our own worlds. The Sunday roast chicken was going to be later than planned.

ON THE RUN

Santiago Chile Marathon

My prayers answered

Ora Pro Nobis

Santiago is a sprawling city of some 5 million souls. It is prone to smog due to pollution and to its location hemmed in between the high Andes and the sea. It has a chequered history in terms of democratic government and is afflicted by areas of severe deprivation. This is not a place that one would normally select to run a marathon.

The main reason for going to Chile was to visit a cousin of mine, Sister Angela McKeever. Angela is a Catholic nun and has lived and worked amongst the poor of Santiago for over 30 years. In her own words, she has 'devoted my life to the people of Chile' and is very likely to end her days there. To me she is 'Mother Angela of Santiago' almost on a parallel with Mother Theresa of Calcutta.

Angela and I shared a similar childhood experience in Ireland. We both spent many years on farms away from our own families. Angela with her aged uncle and aunts and I with my maternal grandmother. We both worked hard on the farm taking on responsibilities way beyond our years. I specialized in milking cows and cattle grazing, Angela in supporting her uncle's greyhound racing enterprise, poultry keeping and gardening – not to mention housework. For me Gaelic Football was a passion and a great outlet for my excess energy and loneliness of living away from my family in London. Angela, apart from attending greyhound meetings, her interests took on a more spiritual dimension, often expressed by long hours of prayer in her local convent school and church. She came from a large family that produced priests, nuns and Christian Brothers aplenty. In those times in Ireland the only alternative to the church or farming or a few chosen professions was emigration. Her elderly aunts were keen for her to be part of the church because it would provide someone to pray for them in this world and in the next.

When I moved to England we lost contact but I did learn that she had become a nun and was in South America. Every few years she returned to Ireland via London and did manage to visit my mother on one or two occasions. As my marathon exploits developed, I made a mental note of getting out to South America to visit her and possibly run a marathon as well. I got her address and telephone number from my mother and was then at last after some 25 years I was able to make contact with her again. I was very impressed with the work that she was doing in Santiago, Chile. She lived amongst and worked with the poor of that city. She provided basic medicines, clothes and spiritual guidance to them. Many women had husbands in prison and she undertook to look after these families as well as visiting the prisoners themselves. In her area, families of 20 or more often lived in just two rooms. Children were out on the streets day and night and the winters can be cold and damp with dense smog. There was drug taking, police raids and sometimes shootings. In this at times mayhem, Angela strode at 5foot tall like a giant, fearless and totally respected by the poor inhabitants to whom she was their servant.

Of all the charities that I have supported over the years, the money that I raised for Angel's work was by far the most cost effective in terms of it use in going directly to providing basic medicines, food and clothing. There were no overheads like some of the big charities that often pocket more than 30% for themselves.

English is not widely spoken in South America. Prior to this trip I spent a year at evening class learning basic Spanish. I also took the opportunity to look up some of the troubled history of South America.

My first inkling that this was going to be a very different experience to my other marathon runs came with registration problems. I paid my registration in US dollars, which was sent by secure named recorded delivery. The name used was one of the organizer of the marathon and I made sure to email him. After some weeks I had heard nothing so I emailed him and he replied that he had received nothing from me. I emailed again to the effect that he had signed for the delivery - this I was able to check separately. Some time later, I resorted to Sister Angel's help and then he claimed that he had only received 'some' of the money – someone else had taken the rest. However - and very generous of him - he would allow me to enter the marathon. When I registered for the marathon in Santiago, I made sure that he met Sister Angel in person. He was a little red faced to say the least. I can only hope he had a lesson on the evils of stealing.

The journey to Santiago proved to be more difficult than I had anticipated. A delayed flight with Iberian Airlines to Madrid meant that I missed my connection to Chile. After some hours at a deserted Madrid airport I talked my way onto a 3am flight to Montevideo in Uruguay – at least it was in South America. We arrived in the middle of a thunderstorm. On getting out of the aircraft in pouring rain, we were greeted with flashes of lightning and tremendous bangs of sound along the perimeter of the airport. Welcome to the next revolution I thought. After more hours of waiting, I got an Argentina Airways plane to Santiago. My dear cousin Sister Angela was there waiting for me. I was the first relative to visit her in South America in over 30 years.

There are two striking things that one notices on first visiting Santiago: wild dogs and buses. The buses are nearly always full. There are hundreds of them and belch out thick black diesel fumes not to mention noise. They form almost a continuous line along the main Avenue Bernado O'Higgins, which is several kilometres long and was part of the route for the marathon course. There are plans to introduce bigger more efficient buses, but at present their fumes and noise pervades the whole city.

There are even more dogs than buses - at least to me it appeared that way. Like the buses, they too would be fellow participants in the marathon. I hope, unlike me, they did not have to register. Despite being wild, the dogs were very friendly and well liked by the inhabitants. They are all interbred to have a uniform size and colouring. On one occasion, I saw a dog and bitch stuck back to back after a love making sessions. Dogs, unlike humans, cannot just roll over after love making. Both dogs looked very sorrowful and forlorn to the amusement of the watching children and adults. On another occasion I saw a bitch sitting very firmly on the ground so as to discourage any amorous attention from other dogs.

Santiago in April can still be hot and humid. I began to worry about the wisdom of running a marathon in this city and noticed that maybe I was not the only one as most of the runners had only entered for the half marathon. My confidence was restored when I realised that I had one of God's representatives on earth supporting me - namely Sister Angela. When I saw how she lived and worked with the poor, travelled on those crowded buses in torrid summers and freezing winters, I realised that her hard working days on the farm in Ireland had in someway prepared her to survive in this city. I had come along way and was not going to let her down now.

On the Sunday morning of the marathon, I headed for the start and Sister Angel head for the church. The starting area was a pleasant enough park- with plenty of dogs of course. There was time to mentally prepare for the task ahead. At 9am, we were on our way. Soon we were out on the main Avenue Bernado O'Higgins. At this point the buses and dogs joined in big time. It was already getting hot and smoggy. The buses had two-thirds of the avenue and the dogs and runners the other one third. The buses went up and down the road showing their support by belching out plumes of black smoke and the occupants of the crowded buses were frantically waving and shouting at us. Did they really want us to join them on the bus?

I began to have second thoughts. Could this be the first marathon that I would not complete? Then I remembered that Sister Angela was praying for me in the church and a spiritual wellbeing came over me. It was a long slow uphill incline for several kilometres towards the invisible Andes in the distance. I now had reached the point of no return and my survival was clearly not entirely in my own hands. I was reliant on spiritual nourishment as well as physical. The dogs and buses became fewer in number and I began to feel at last that I was in a marathon- even more so when most of the runners peeled away towards the half- marathon finish.

My training for this marathon as usual broke most of the guidelines for marathon running- mostly I do much too little. I nearly always spend February half-term skiing in Austria and the Easter holiday skiing in Norway – my wife's country. Some of my runs are on snow and it can be very cold but at least the air is fresh. As this marathon was in mid–April, I did not have too much time to run in England before leaving for South

America. I still am fortunate to be able to keep a reservoir of fitness and stamina to call on as I train all year round.

After about 15km I met up with a Canadian in his mid-thirties who I noticed was carrying his wallet and passport in his left hand. I got talking to him and he told me that he was staying in a Youth Hostel and did not want to take the risk of leaving his valuables at the Hostel. He had previously run a marathon in Nairobi in Kenya and deployed a similar technique there. In my book to run 42 km holding a largish wallet in your hand is an achievement in itself.

He was hoping to get round in under 4 hours, a similar target to mine, and as there were so few marathon runners it seemed a good idea to run together. After 30km, we turned for home to head down Avenue Bernado O'Higgins and rejoin our fellow dogs and buses. By now, the traffic had increased and there was a police officer and another man with a red flag at each intersection. The real fun was about to begin.

As we approached an intersection, it looked as though nothing was going to stop those determined Chilean drivers. We were getting tired by now and one had to concentrate on just keeping running. Often we were only meters away from the cars when they were finally brought to a stop by frantic waving of the red flag and the raising of the police officer's baton and the simultaneous blowing on his traffic whistle, As we crossed, we were greeted by a crescendo of hooting car horns. At first, I thought that this was a Chilean motorist way of supporting the runners. On second thoughts, I was not so sure as I experienced a similar control system in the last 10km of the Athens marathon. Then I knew for sure that the Athenian motorists do not like obstacles of any description in their way.

Towards the finish, we passed the Chilean National Football Stadium. This stadium was used for purposes other than football and pop concerts under the Augusto Pinochet regime in the 1980s. Under his military dictatorship, thousands of people were held in the stadium before finally disappearing. Neighbouring Argentina used similar methods around the same period.

My Canadian partner stayed with me until the last 2km when I slowly pulled away from him but by then I knew he would achieve his target of less than 4 hours. I finished in a time of 3hr 49 min - a miracle given the circumstances. Clearly Sister Angela's prayerful intervention had worked.

I sometimes try to get a second medal from the finishing marshals if someone has been supportive of my efforts. I am pleased to state that Sister Angela's Santiago marathon medal is proudly on display next to a crucifix in her lounge. For Sister Angela life is a spiritual marathon and when she crosses the finishing line at the gates to heaven, I am sure that race marshal St Peter will present her with her heavenly medal.

The next day we were able to visit some of the homes of people where Sister Angela lives and performs her earthly tasks.

Despite their obvious poverty, I was impressed by the dignity and pride of many of the people I met. One particular family that I met was headed by a Mapuche Indian women who was married to a local man from Santiago of Spanish descent. She was proud of her many children and of her Indian origin. Sister Angela translated her answers to my questions about the Mapuche Indians.

For centuries the Mapuche owned most of the lands in south Chile. The Spanish Conquistadors set about taking these lands much as their north European counterparts in North America. The Mapuche were partially successful in their resistance and there are still one million Mapuche out of a total population of fifteen million Chileans. Part of the conquered lands contains a monoculture of extensive forests that gives little work to the Mapuche. The wood is exported to the US and Europe yielding great profits for the local big landowners. In the 1880s, after further violent military expeditions, the Mapuche Nation was incorporated into the state of Chile. A lot of Mapuche were transferred to reservations to live in abject poverty. The dictator Augusto Pinochet to suppress Mapuche rebellions used anti-terrorist laws. Sadly under the current more democratic set up the laws are still employed to continue to deprive the Mapuche of their lands and living. The Mapuche lady of the house showed me her Indian headdress and some photographs of her in full Mapuche dress when she lived in her homeland. I even got a chance to play the Mapuche drums. All I can say is what I said in that house. Viva La Mapuche. A week later I visited Argentina on my way home and noticed that there were few native Indians left in that country.

Part of the title for this section included 'Ora pro Nobis' which means pray for us. Thank you Sister Angela for all those prayers and may you continue with the wonderful work that you are doing for the poor of Chile.

Update 2019

I met up with Sister Angela in Ireland last year just after her retirement from her mission to Chile. She misses Chile and I am sure the poor of Santiago miss her even more. She intends to go to Mexico for a few months to help comfort and support the refugees escaping the drug gangs in Central America.

Berlin Marathon 1990

Backs to the Wall

Of all my marathons, this one had the most emotional start and was historically for me on a par with the running of the 100th Boston marathon. Berlin on several occasions has been the fault line between freedom and oppression. One recalls: the Hitler Berlin Olympics and the marching Nazi columns through its streets; the famous photograph of a Soviet soldier placing the Red Flag of Communism on the roof of the burnt out German Reichstag building; the memorable speech of President Kennedy in West Berlin next to the wall saying 'Ich bin ein Berliner' and the visit of Barack Obama in 2008 speaking for a free world where people of all races can live and work.

In 1989, the first cracks began to appear in the wall that divided Berlin. The wall formed part of what Churchill termed the 'Iron Curtain' that stretched from the Baltic to the Balkans. It was the front line in the cold war between two ideologies: collective communism and individual capitalism. Unfortunately Soviet style communism was a big departure from the communism envisaged by Karl Marx and it had to depend on totalitarianism and control of the individual's rights of free speech and movement.

Soon the cracks became gaps allowing the free movement between East and West Berlin. The cold war was over. Prior to 1990, the marathon only took place in West Berlin with the symbolic start at the wall itself – literally, the runners had their backs to the wall. This time it would be very different. Now the start was about a mile from the wall and we would run towards the Brandenburg Gate and into East Berlin. In the words

73

of Hugh Jones the 1982 London marathon winner and pacemaker for this race: 'We came from all corners of the world, 25,000 runners from 60 countries competing in the first all Berlin marathon since the 1936 Olympic marathon in the city….We received a tumultuous reception from spectators as we emerged into East Berlin from the Brandenburg Gate. Five miles later, we were making an uncomfortable return to the west. The remnants of the wall were under our feet, hostility hastily buried under a patchy layer of tarmac.' The front pages of the world's press captured the historic moment as the runners ran through the Brandenburg Gate. I vividly remember a bank of hundreds of photographers waiting in the middle of the wide road for our entry. I recall the tall soviet built TV tower that had acted as a big brother symbol to keep Eastern Europe in check. Along the bleak open streets of East Berlin there was sullenness in some of the local residents and East German guards. It was still 3 days before official reunification on the 3rd October and I have a lasting impression of the drab prefab concrete flats and the odd fibreglass Trabant cars parked along the streets. The early yellow-brown autumn leaves were swirling in the breeze around the pavements and there was a strange grey eerie emptiness, which in turn induced a silence in all the runners. It was as if this autumn decay was symbolising the end of the old communist regime and its cruel absolute power over the people.

Back through no man's land and towards the west our spirits began to lift and as the number of spectators increased it began to feel that we were at last running a big city marathon. As we ran the long trek past the Zoological gardens towards Kurfurstendamm, the commercial centre of West Berlin, I recognised the streets that my wife and I had to walk alone in the early hours of the morning of the previous day.

My wife as a teacher of German wanted to experience East Berlin before things became too westernized. On the Friday morning, we took a train to Alexanderplatz in the heart of old Berlin. As we walked along the famous Unter den Lindern towards the Opera House, I was reminded of the decadent Berlin of the 1930s as depicted in the film Der Blaue Engel and starring Marlene Dietrich. At the Opera House, we were able to book box office tickets for the evening performance of La Traviata for only £5 a seat. Whilst trying to book the tickets I was ignored by the two women in the booking office whose morning chat was more important than attending to customers. I did let them know in German that they would be in for a bit of a shock when capitalism took hold in the east. I think that they must have been intoxicated by their newfound wealth when the Ost mark was converted overnight to the same value as the Deutsh Mark. Like their fellow East Germans they would soon come to realise that capitalism can have no gain without pain. Later we went to a nearby café and met some older East Germans. Some of them had a pre war naval background and we were astonished to find that they were expressing Old Prussian Teutonic values of superiority and it was as if communism never happened. After this surprise we decided to get a train and go a few kilometres deeper into East Berlin to hopefully meet some 'real' East Berliners. A few stops along the line we saw some very large complex of beehive shaped blocks of flats and decided to visit them. As we drew near we noticed that there was a café in the basement of one of the blocks and decided to go in and order a coupe of beers. One customer on hearing us speak English rushed over, introduced himself as a lecturer from the local further education college, and said that we were the first people that he had met from the West. To celebrate the special occasion he insisted that we share a bottle of fine Crimean champagne with him and as my wife speaks very good German, it was not long before this man revealed his life story. In doing so we drank two more bottles of Champagne but at least we got to pay for one of them. He told us that he lectured in motor mechanics and he realised that Trabant two stroke engine cars would not be quiet able to compete with Porsche and Mercedes technology, so the future work wise for him was bleak but he looked forward to the new freedom and the opportunity for travel and retraining in the West.

Needless to state we arrived well inebriated and late for the opera, and duly stumbled into our box seats. I cannot image what such seats would have cost at Covent Garden in London. After the opera we decided to sober up a bit and visit a café where we got in more conversation and at midnight we left to get a train to take us back the 5kilometers or so to West Berlin. To our surprise we found the station was closed and there was only one option for us – a long walk back through no man's land to the West. We walked past the empty Reichstag and through the Brandenburg gate. There were few people and no cars around and soon we were completely alone and isolated between East and West Berlin It was extraordinary to contemplate that we would be one of the last people to experience the desolation of landscape and suppression of free speech and movement that represented the cold war. In just over 24 hours, 25,000 runners would be running on the very road that we were now standing on and soon after that there would be traffic and human movement on this main reopened road night and day in the future. We got to our hotel around 3.30am and Saturday was definitely going to be a day of rest.

As for the marathon itself, I was fully rested by Sunday morning. The weather was cool, cloudy and dry, ideal condition for running. I was able to finish the race in 3hr 28 min as expected. Afterwards my wife and I enjoyed our first Japanese meal served in traditional surroundings and style; but before that of course I managed a couple of Guinness in an Irish Pub.

Our flight home was delayed by two hours and we arrived in London when the tubes and trains were closed so it was a taxi ride to my parent's flat in North London. My wife and I got up very early on Monday morning to join the mad rush to get to our respective schools and soon our trip to Berlin was just a distant memory; but one that will stay with us for the rest of our days.

Today - 2019 – the Berlin Marathon is one of the world's premier marathons. The world marathon record has been broken eight times in Berlin; the last was 2018 with a time of 2hour 1min39sec. The sub two hour marathon is getting ever closer.

Ja, Ich bin ein Berliner.

The Path to Rome

In my teens I was introduced by my brother-in-law to a book titled 'The Path to Rome' written in the 19C by Hilaire Belloc. His journey was a spiritual Odyssey. He was enriched by his interactions with different people and places as he walked through eastern France, Germany, Switzerland, over the Alps and along the Apennines down into Rome. He made his walk that bit more challenging by taking the shortest and most direct route to Rome as well as trying to attend Mass every day.

As for me, I was attracted by a walk or even a bike ride to Rome rather than just flying there and savouring the idea of a bit of an adventure with the spiritual dimension being a possible bonus.

My journey to Rome happened when least expected and the path was a very different route to that taken by Belloc.

As mentioned elsewhere, we have some very close German friends that we first met in Germany in 1977. The very first Germans that we befriended were a lovely young German couple, with a beautiful baby girl called Christina, who were finishing their studies at Bonn University. They helped us to acquire their student flat to accommodate my wife and two sons for their year long stay while my wife studied at the University. Some years later a very attractive blond 16-year-old German girl – namely Christina – stayed with us as part of a six month placement in the sixth form of a local school. A few years later her mother and father visited us as part of a tour round England. Christina's father Ludwin had arranged some short stay exchanges between students at his college and my own school in Berkhamstead. On one such visit just before Easter 1996, Ludwin, whilst staying with us, offered the use of a caravan that he was going to take to a beautiful campsite at Anguillara along Lake Bracciano just 16 miles north

79

of Rome. This offer was by way of a thank you for the school partnership exchanges and for having his daughter in our home.

Rome! The memory of Belloc's 'Path to Rome' book came flooding back to me. I told Ludwin that I had always wanted to go to Rome but it had never been my intention to fly or drive there. Still I was not going to turn down the offer of free accommodation on a campsite just a short bus ride from the eternal city. A couple of weeks later I went to Boston, America, to participate in the 100th running of that city's marathon. When I got back home in the early evening as dusk was falling, I picked up a letter in my hallway with unusual black lines around the edge of the envelope and a German postmark. I opened it. I was shocked to read in German that Ludwin had died age 46 years old. He had been born with a slight congenital heart defect and during the Easter vacation had felt unwell and was taken to hospital where he died within 24 hours of admission probably due to a viral infection of the heart.

Some weeks passed until I spoke to his very distraught wife Hannah – theirs had been a marriage made in heaven- and she suggested that we could take the caravan which had been recently purchased in Germany to Rome as the very popular campsite had been booked. A little later it was decided that we would come to their home town of Aachen to collect the caravan and take Hannah's youngest children aged 11 and 13 with us to Rome. Hannah would fly out later to join us. So this was going to be my path to Rome.

It seemed strange to spend one's summer holiday with a grieving family. It was very difficult to know how to relieve the constant pain of grief, particularly for Hannah. We went to some open air concerts and on occasion I walked along the lakeside with her. Although the area brought back memories for Hannah of the lovely summers spent here with her husband and family, it was also comforting for her to be in a place where she shared so many happy moments with Ludwin. There was a particular high point of this trip that occurred when we visited St Peters. On Hannah's advice, we took the early bus into Rome and were first in the queue to get into the Sistine Chapel. Hannah told me to go ahead and follow the signs – quite a long way- to get to the Chapel and I arrived in the Chapel five minutes before anyone else. I lay down on the floor and spent several minutes looking up at Michelangelo's famous Sistine Ceiling in spiritual bliss. The outstretched finger of the hand of God just touching the upwards stretching index finger on the hand of Adam offering him the gift of life was very moving. Some time later it occurred to me that this image reflected the now heavenly and spiritual love between Hannah and Ludwin. Later we walked up the Cupola to get a magnificent view of the hills of Rome and of Ancient Rome. I looked northwards towards Britain and Ireland and thought of Belloc walking all that way on his own over a hundred years ago.

In 1996 our daughter Astrid was 10 years old. She had made friends with an older Italian girl called Julia from Rome at the campsite. Three years later Astrid and I would be back in the Eternal City not only to meet Julia but for Astrid to do her first competitive 5km run and for me to run the Rome Marathon. This time we would be going by plane as we only had the week-end off as this was school term time.

We got in to Rome late on Saturday evening and after avoiding some dodgy taxi drivers eventually got an 'official city taxi' - even then the driver still managed to overcharge us – to our hotel 'The Pyramids', an unusual name for a hotel in Rome but the city did owe a lot to the cultures of Egypt and Greece. Luckily, Julia's father picked up our race numbers, as we were late for registration.

We were up early on Sunday morning and were pleased to meet Julia in the Hotel lobby as she smoked her second cigarette of the day. We walked to the Colosseum and it was not long before Astrid and I were off on our 5km and 42km runs respectively. Both races started and finished at the Colosseum. After Astrid finished her race Julia took her sightseeing and for lunch in her apartment near the Vatican.

The weather was very pleasant with a starting temperature of about 18Celsius and sunny. It did get a little warmer as the morning progressed so a very good marathon time was not on the menu for me. The course was essentially a single lap taking in most of the great sights of new and ancient Rome. We started in front of the Colosseum, down the Via Cavour, past the ancient Forum to the Piazza del Papollo and across the Tiber to St Peter's Square. Then along the Tiber past the 1972 Olympic Stadium along the Via del Foro Italico to again cross the Tiber and come back to Villa Ada, past the Stadio Flaminia and again to the Piazza del Popolo. Next to the Spanish Steps, the Trevi Fountain – no time to throw any coins in - the famous Pantheon, around the Colosseum, past the Circus Maximus, past The English Graveyard – burial place of the English poet John Keats past the Pyramids (close to our hotel of the same name) to San Paulo and then back up again past the Ancient Baths to finish next to the Colosseum. The course was a journey through Rome down the centuries taking in most of the key attractions and probably the most cultural and historical route of all the marathons that I have run so far.

Some memorable moments included the enthusiastic clapping of the runners as we ran through the narrow Via Del Corso which returned the compliment by echoing back with several reverberations and as we ran into the Piazza Navona with the Pantheon in front of us we got so close to the waiters, who were weaving their way through the runners to serve the outdoor customers, that I had to resist the temptation of taking a quick espresso off one of their trays. Mind you, it would have cost less as you pay less for a coffee in Rome if you take it standing up. I got to the half way in 1hr 51min; a little slow for me but enjoying the scenic run was much more important than trying to beat my personal clock. As the temperature increased, I began to struggle a bit more and was glad that I had decided to run in shorts and thin running vest. I can always measure my heat output by how many times I have to wring the sweat out of my headband and by the end it was getting to be about every 3 minutes, yes I was getting really hot. It was strange that I should be passing the Circus Maximus and then the longish run to the Colosseum when I was suffering the most as these two places in ancient times saw great suffering and even death from the competitions that they engaged in to satisfy the more sadistic needs of the Roman citizens and their Emperors.

I finished in 3hr 47 min but the whole experience of this run was the abiding memory for me, rather than my time. My daughter Astrid had a very good 5km run and felt that she could have run much faster which is always a good feeling and hope for the next run. After a rest in my hotel Astrid and Julia came back to the hotel and we went out for a bit more sight seeing this time with a born and bred Roman. Julia took us to an ancient street that bore her name and later we dined in a true Italian restaurant where my daughter was serenaded by a very enthusiastic musician. Whilst we enjoyed the Italian cuisine our musician was satisfied that 'music was the food of love' and some money of course. Soon it was arrivederci to

Julia and time for the flight back to London and school for both of us on Monday morning.

Later in the week, the local paper had a headline 'End of the Road for School's Marathon Man'. I was due to end my career as a full-time teacher in senior management and take up new opportunities in the private sector. In my 11 years at this school, I had started with the Athens marathon and finished with the Rome marathon going from one ancient city to another. I was not giving up running of course as quoted in the my local paper. You can't give up running. You have to keep on going. It is in the blood. Even if you have to crawl around the course. Now in 2019 I still hold the same opinion.

The path to Rome for me has taken many forms and enhanced my life in many unexpected ways and will always be associated with the death of Ludwin –R.I.P.

The Long Par 5

One of the advantages of retirement is that you have more time, and more money, to take up sporting and social activities that eluded you due to work commitments.

Probably the "sport" that many seniors plumb for in retirement is golf. Joining a golf club gives the opportunity to spend up to four hours on a round of golf in the open air in pleasant surroundings and the chance to keep your waistline in trim. There is the added attraction of occasionally making some birdies, the odd eagle and the holy grail of a hole in one. Of course if the golf round is not going too well there is the opportunity to see some real live birds around most golf course. We seem to have an abundance of red kites flying over my Hertfordshire golf course.

A golfer who carries their club bag can expect to expend more calories than a rugby player does during a full rugby match. The mental challenge of having to make the correct choice of club and strategy for almost every stroke played could help to stave off the onset of dementia and other illnesses. Golf courses tend to have less air pollution and contribute to reducing global warming. At the end of the 19th Century, the rapid growth of golf clubs in and around cities helped to stem the expansion of urban sprawl in the 20th Century. The many golf clubs - over 70 - in our capital city has contributed to make it one of the greenest cities in the world.

There are downsides to golfing. Some believe that golfing is the best way to spoil a good walk. Some seniors become addicted to golf and in consequence leave their partners to sample premature widowhood. Some spend more time at the 19th hole than the playing on the previous 18 holes.

Then there is the physical aspect of golf. Like most games, the skills needed to play good golf are best acquired when young. The game requires flexibility, balance, good timing and visualization. Unfortunately, many seniors are overweight, lack suppleness, have poor vision and are on their second or even third hip and knee replacements.

During my teaching career, I kept fit by playing football, squash and managed to get in some runs helping with the school cross-country. The idea of spending more than four hours on a round of golf was out of the question; but I did hold on to the idea of playing some golf when I got old and maybe buy a decent set of golf clubs if I achieved a reasonable club handicap. Well, I have now achieved the first target but with a handicap of 20 and age over seventy years, I still feel that I am not yet ready to treat myself to any expensive golf clubs.

For years golf clubs were very exclusive and this was very off putting - no pun intended - to those of us who would like to try out a round of golf when younger. I am pleased that golf clubs have become far more welcoming to new club members and occasional golfers. Golf societies, even local pub societies are now actively welcomed.

Life on the golf course can be a daunting experience for high handicap seniors. Even for professionals it is not easy to hit a 4cm golf ball with a 115cm long club resting in a divot on the fairway, never mind hitting the ball out of long wet grass off the fairway. Recently at my club we played our third round of our winter league on a frost covered course. Pitching a ball onto the green was as if playing it onto a concrete car park and watching it bounce off the green into the frozen rough. There was one up side though. I got a great bounce off a frozen lake right onto the green behind. Professional golfers would never play in such conditions. It is ironic that the high handicapper will find themselves playing out of woods, long grass, scrub and very poor lies that professionals rarely get into in the first place.

The frustration and anger I have seen from some seniors is almost "heart stopping". Golf clubs are broken or thrown into lakes in anger and some even walking off the course in disgust. The swearing ability of the frustrated amateur has to be heard to be believed.

Golfers and seniors have their foibles aplenty. Some will spend ages looking for a tee that cost less than one penny. Others will continue to look for lost balls in bushes even when they have found their own ball. Others will take the opportunity to fish spare balls out of streams and lakes. I once saved a senior's life when he fell in a deep lake lined with slimy plastic trying to fetch a ball that was not even his own!

Then there is the search for that magical single figure handicap or at least one less than 20. No expense is spared when it comes to buying that special club or series of golf lessons that will help – hopefully - lower their handicap.

The rules of golf as set down by The Royal and Ancient still continue to be beyond my mental grasp. What do you do when your ball is under, or near to, a rake in a bunker? What do you do in the same situation when the rake is left outside the bunker? Can one always differentiate between a movable and an immovable object and on it goes.

Heart attacks are not uncommon on a golf course. My mother got Bing Crosby's autograph in 1977 when she met him by chance playing on her local golf course – Mill Hill in north London. Bing was a keen golfer and played in The British and American Amateur Championships off a handicap of 2. A few days later he played a full round of golf in Spain and dropped dead from a massive heart attack when returning to the clubhouse. However, playing golf can also alert you to potential heart problems. Sometime later, my mother in her 60s, was walking up a long par 5 at Mill Hill and felt a bit out of breath. She asked her playing partner if she was also feeling out of breath but she was not. Not long after she had her mitral valve fixed and a heart pacemaker inserted. She continued to have many more years of golfing.

A final thought for all seniors on a tight budget. Recently I played in our annual Christmas 3 club + putter competition. I scored Stapleford 35 points off a handicap of 20 using a driver, 7-fairway wood and 8 iron. Two weeks earlier I achieved 3rd place in the well attended Seniors' Winter Shield with 37 points using nearly a full set of golf clubs. No, I will not be buying new clubs anytime soon. In fact I may well lighten my bag of some clubs and carry some more bananas instead – good for the heart, especially on a long par 5.

The Comeback London Marathon, April 2014 – Put on Your Ipods Please – All Plugged in and Ready for the Off.

It was three years since my last marathon in Milan in 2011 and two years since my double heart bypass at The Royal Brompton in London. It was a great feeling as I cycled to catch the 7.15 am train from Hertford to London to run in the 34th London Marathon. It was 30 years since my first ever marathon - the fourth running of the London in 1984. I was back in the running game.

However, a host of known unknowns curtailed my excitement. Would my sore Achilles and calf muscles hold up? Would the effort aggravate my sore groin and tender lower back problems? Above all, would my heart take the strain? I did know that this marathon was going to be a very different experience than what I had already encountered in running 55 marathons in 30 countries.

Why the Heart Bypass?

In 1988, I ran my first international marathon in Paris in aid of CORDA, a charity supporting research into coronary heart disease at The Royal Brompton Hospital in London. Little did I realise that in 2012 I would need the services of this hospital for a life saving double heart bypass.

In 2010 on our annual ski trip to Austria, I noticed that I was struggling to complete my usual after ski runs and put this down to getting on in age and running at high altitude. I did manage to walk up on skies the Kitzbueler Horn – a vertical height of one kilometre- but had to stop at regular intervals as others walked past me to my great annoyance. At Easter 2011, I completed the Milan marathon in 4 hours 23 minutes - my slowest time ever. I put this down to the hot conditions - it was about 27 C at the finish. Some months later, I was struggling to keep running for three or more kilometres without having to walk, recover and then get going again. I had no problem completing moderate swimming sessions and bicycle tours of 2 or 3 hours. It was the extra energy required to run that was my problem. I realised that there had to be some sort of heart problem and instigated a series of heart tests. I had good ECG and Echocardiogram results. A CTC scan showed a little above normal calcification of part of my coronary system. Finally, my consultant who was very interested in solving the problem performed an angiogram and even he was surprised with the result. He discovered a 99% blockage at the junction leading to two out of the three main coronary branches. He was amazed that I had no pain at rest never mind when I was running. He made the decision there and then to detain me in hospital. Five days later, I had my bypass at the Royal Brompton.

Some of my maternal uncles had died in their fifties from heart problems; but they were smokers and quite heavy drinkers. My father died at 88 years and my mother is still alive at 92 years- although she did have a mitral valve heart problem for over twenty years. My siblings have had no heart problems so I was the one who drew the genetic short straw. If I had not noticed the deterioration in my running ability and had a more sedentary life style, my first heart attack would almost certainly have killed me. The medical profession refer to my particular heart disease as 'the widow maker'.

The build up to the marathon.

In August 2012, during the London Olympics, and three months after my bypass, I had a bit of a setback. Although jogging again I was finding it hard going and was suffering from breathlessness. My blood pressure monitor showed that I had an irregular heartbeat. An ECG revealed that I had atrial flutter. My heart was like a car engine misfiring and it was no wonder I found jogging difficult. My cardiologist booked me in for a cardio- version and I managed to avoid the dreaded Warfarin- with its blood tests and limits on my beer intake – in favour of a new drug that did allow me to carry on imbibing the amber nectar. I was back to running again before Christmas and in February I again ski climbed the Kitzbular Horn without having to stop too often. I completed my first competitive race - a 10km - in April 2011 in about 60 minutes.

I carried on with my usual pattern of training: walking, golfing - I carry my own gear-some swimming, short gym workouts and two or three 5km runs on grass weekly. By August, I thought it would be appropriate to enter for an autumn half-marathon and found one in Brentwood, Essex in late October – nice and flat as well. After Camping in the south of France and keeping to my usual training pattern with the addition of daily wine supplies, I was ready for my half- marathon. On re-reading my entry details I noticed that the race was titled "The Brentwood Ultra Half-Marathon" and was a six lap race including three long climbs per lap and some very muddy paths through woods – not at all what I had expected. On the morning of the race, the remnants of Hurricane Julian had arrived. I just about survived the ordeal recording a time of 2 Hr 25 Min, my worst time ever for this distance; but it was also the toughest race that I have run at this distance and I had achieved my final step to a full marathon.

It was too late to enter the lottery for the London Marathon. I wanted to run a marathon in the UK to reduce insurance costs and to benefit from the services of a free NHS in the event of things going wrong during the race. It was still possible to get into the London marathon by supporting a charity and I contacted The Thomas Coram Foundation, now known as

Coram. I had helped set up their London marathon gold entry scheme in the 1990s and had run for them on several occasions. Unfortunately, they had already allocated their marathon places but it was good to know that they were still fully involved with the marathon. The Coram is the world's oldest incorporated charity and has strong links with Handel, Hogarth and other former London notables. Success came my way when Cheshire Disability (of Leonard Cheshire fame) gave me a place provided I raised a minimum of £2000 for this worthy cause.

I now had less than four months to get in shape with the added challenge of 3 weeks in Singapore and Vietnam – visiting our daughter – and 2 weeks in Austria following in my wife's ski tracks! I managed to swim nearly every day whilst visiting our daughter but managed only three runs in the extreme heat. Running in Austria at high altitude was tough but beneficial, but my beer and wine intake on the ski slopes was increased. During March, I was able to do my normal routine of golfing, running, walking, swimming and some gym short sessions that also included bike workouts. My longest total weekly mileage was two weeks of about 26 miles and my longest run was a session lasting 2 hours 35 minutes on grass paths. I am fortunate to be able to achieve fair marathon times for my age and weight - 68 years old and 75 Kgm - on a much lower mileage than most other runners are. I think that this is the reason along with cross training that my joints are still ok.

I registered for the marathon at the O2 centre, next to the Thames in East London. There I had the pleasure of having my photo taken with one of the greatest modern day distance runners Haile Gebrselassie. He recently held the world record for the marathon and is a multi gold medal winner in Olympic and world championship events. He was the pace maker for the marathon.

Marathon Day

Arose at 6.10 am and had my usual porridge and banana. Well Vaselined and kitted up, I cycled to catch the 7.15 am train from Hertford to Charing Cross on a glorious sunny day. I bought a strong coffee and the Sun newspaper – very light reading only required – and boarded my train. Sitting opposite was a fellow runner. This tall amateur rugby player was participating in his first marathon and was sorting out his iPod. He told me he had loaded up 60 songs/tunes for his run. It was clear to me that he thought that he needed this music to motivate him to get round the course. Of all the big city marathons that I have run, London is well ahead when it comes to crowd support and fancy dress - not to mention the Pearly Queens and Kings. I told this young man that there would be nearly a million spectators cheering him on and he would not need any motivation from his music, which would in fact cut him off from both his fellow runners and the spectators. He would miss the random interactions and real joy of running The London. He listened but I think he had already made up his mind to plug himself in to the music world of his own making. He was not to be the only one. I estimate that 30% to 40% of the runners were plugged into their iPods. I did my best to get some runners to unplug and engage in some banter and hear the crowd support; but I am afraid I could not hold back the iPod tide.

At Oxford Circus, we met a runner from Yorkshire all ready to run with no extra kit and hoping to break 3 hours - tough chaps these Northerners. There was no sign of any iPod on him. His previous best was 3.05.

I arrived about 45 minutes before the start and had time for a photo with The Banana Man and another with the Lion King. I always like a strong coffee before the start to sort out the build up of lactic acid later on in the race – well I think it works after a fashion. A last call came over the antennae for all runners to put their kit bags on the lorries and I quickly put my coffee aside and rushed over to my designated area. Later I realised I had left my Vaseline, suntan cream and eye drops in my kit bag which did not augur too well for my final preparations. It had been three years since my last marathon in Milan, so I had forgotten aspects of my normal prerace routine. I did manage to borrow some Vaseline from a runner who was putting it on their eyebrows – great idea to stop the sweat going into your eyes. Why did it take me thirty years to learn this?

Because of my uncertainty about how I was going to fare in this race, I started near the back of the red start – with about 20,000 runners in front of me. This turned out to be a big mistake. I soon realised this when I had to step sideways to get past slower runners. I passed a man carrying a fridge after about 3miles. He was wise enough to start towards the front and let other runners pass him. My mistake would catch up with me around the 18-mile mark.

As usual there was great crowd support and it was a lovely day if a little on the hot side. I was very impressed with the number of runners supporting charitable causes, some very personal. One woman that I talked to – not plugged in – told me that she was supporting a liver transplant charity. Her mother had a liver transplant twenty years previously at age 38. She said the only sign that anything was wrong was her mother's yellow skin colour. An Irish girl from Cork was running for breast cancer research in honour of her mother who died from the disease. I noticed a young woman wearing a Delmelza Hospice for Children T-shirt. In 2003, I ran the Budapest marathon for this charity. I managed to get her to unplug her iPod to have a chat. I also had a chat with a police officer whose running vest had the words 'I want anarrest' emblazoned on it. A cheerful Canadian couple were running London because they had heard about the great atmosphere.

I estimated that over 90% of runners were running for charity. In my first London marathon in 1984, a minority of the runners ran for charity. There was also a very big increase in the number of women runners. One welcome IT development was the ability to track the progress of each runner. My daughter was able to do this from Singapore; but my wife who I hoped to see near Canary Wharf found the system was overloaded.

Just after The Cutty Sark, I was pleased to see The Cheshire Disability supporters and that extra cheer sent me on my way to Tower Bridge. I was happy with my pace but had the continuing problem of having to step sideways to pass slower runners. The soles of my feet were getting sore with this unusual sideways movement. I was hoping that no blisters would develop. I was very surprised how crowded it was even from mile 17 onwards. It was difficult to see the road ahead to avoid stepping on empty bottles. I was pleasantly surprised when a woman runner introduced herself to me. She recognised my Cheshire Disability running vest and told me she had run the marathon for them the previous year. She lived near one of their homes in the north of England. I then saw her falling sideways towards the kerb and managed to grab her. Other runners tried to avoid us and we nearly had one of those mass crashes that you see in

The Tour de France bike race. She had stepped on a rolling unseen empty lucazade bottle.

My soles of my feet were very sore by mile 18. I was still sure that I had no blisters and I knew what was needed was a bit more cushioning. Luckily, I saw a St John's ambulance station and asked them to stick some bandaging into my socks. Five minutes later I was off and running on air. Job done. At the Tower of London, I met the Cheshire Disability supporters again. I also waved to crowds on an overhead bridge and got a tremendous 'You can do it Sean' response. I had my name 'Sean' printed front and back on my running vest and felt almost as popular as Shaun the Sheep.

The Tower of London has been a place of torture and incarceration down the centuries and at this section of the race I was hitting my own Wall of torture. Achilles tendons were beginning to play up a bit, odd pangs of pain in calves and kidney area. Was I beginning to fall apart? Would my bypasses burst? Sorry too much negative thinking. Stay positive. Yes, we can!

I could see the Houses of Parliament in the distance. I now found myself with a runner from South Africa - he asked me to take a photo of him with Parliament in the background whilst still running. He told me he had run the Comrades ultra marathon in SA. I wondered how he had so much energy left. I wanted to tell him to run on ahead but I could not – 'keep going Sean' I said to myself. Going up Birdcage Walk, he wanted another selfie and one of the two of us with Buckingham Palace in the background whilst still running. I have never finished a marathon like this before. Then we sprinted up the Mall - I think I just got over the line before him – but it did not matter. He then wanted another photo of the two of us at the finish.

I had made it and in a time of 4 hours 40 minutes plus my 5 minutes at The St John's station. The body had held together. The Cheshire Disability was £2500 better off and my wife and daughter badly needed a cup of tea.

Postscript

In 2015 I decided to enter for a different type of marathon – The 100 Mile Olympic Legacy Bike Ride in support of Cystic Fibrosis and this time I had my son to guide me. However, I still had the running bug and after another Lottery rejection, ran the London 2016 marathon again for Cheshire Disability. Despite sore feet problems, I finished in 4 hours 42 minutes.

In 2017 I had some more heart problems to do with bradycardia and AF – a very slow resting heart rate and atrial flutter. I ended up back again at the Royal Brompton, London for a heart ablation operation. My consultant was pleased with the success of the operation and later gave me the go ahead to run another marathon.

I discovered that my 2016 London marathon time gave me automatic entry for the 2018 marathon on a good time for age basis and no need for a lottery entry. It transpired that the 2018 marathon was the hottest day in the marathon's history. As it turned out my sore feet were my biggest problem. I needed three stops for feet repairs with the St John's Ambulance people and a big thank you to them all. I finished in 5 hours 23 minutes which was my slowest ever marathon; but not too bad for a 72 year old bloke I suppose. Excluding the three stops, my actually running time was still less than 5 hours. There was a positive aspect to my efforts — I was able to donate more than £1000 sponsorship money towards my ablation cardiologist's state of the art new heart scanner.

CPSIA information can be obtained
at www.ICGtesting.com
Printed in the USA
BVHW031057150819
555976BV00005B/60/P